Dimensions of Broadcast Editorializing

No. 697
$8.95

Dimensions of Broadcast Editorializing

By Edd Routt

PN
4778
R64

TAB BOOKS
Blue Ridge Summit, Pa. 17214

FIRST EDITION

FIRST PRINTING— MARCH 1974

Copyright © 1974 by TAB BOOKS

Printed in the United States
of America

Reproduction or publication of the content in any manner, without express permission of the publisher, is prohibited. No liability is assumed with respect to the use of the information herein.

Hardbound Edition: International Standard Book No. 0-8306-3697-8

Library of Congress Card Number: 73-89816

Preface

This text encouraging broadcasters to write and air more and stronger editorials was prepared in 1971-72, a period in which the communication media were beset by harsh and powerful critics. Reporters were being jailed on contempt of court charges after refusing to divulge news sources. White House spokesmen were recommending that station licensees be held responsible for network newscast content. Licensees were still plagued by strike applicants and Congress voted for itself bottom rates for members' political advertising.

Travis Linn's introduction to this book refers to licensee reluctance to editorialize and looks to the time when broadcast editorials will be as commonplace as broadcast news. Sol Taishoff of **Broadcasting** magazine, years ago, exhorted licensees to take up the cudgel and defend themselves with strong, bold editorials. Most broadcasters will give lip service to the need for effective editorializing, but comparatively few have recognized opinion-giving as a vital part of their broadcast service.

Most of the material for this text was derived from original research. No panacea was sought or even hoped for; a first step in textbooks for broadcast editorials was hoped for and hopefully has been achieved. A complete list of contributors is contained in the back of the book, but special expressions of appreciation are due Bob Manewith of WGN, Chicago, and Travis Linn of WFAA-TV, Dallas. Sandra Cohen of Bloom Advertising and Kitty Norwood of the Southland Corporation, both Dallas, served as research assistant and local editor, respectively. Both are deeply involved in human communications in the fields of advertising and education.

Norma Routt, the infinitely more patient side of the author's household, edited and typed the manuscript. Gordon

McLendon, a life-long friend, offered sage advice and much encouragement. In addition to providing some solid experiences, most of the contributors wrote side notes that encouraged the author to bring the work to fruition. Some very busy executives, such as Peter Straus of WMCA, spent considerable time finding answers to my many questions. Many less-busy executives were too busy to be bothered.

This book, if it is to be dedicated to anyone, should be dedicated to the licensee who has recognized and taken a community leadership role for himself and his station, and to the student who enters broadcasting believing the medium has a social duty beyond entertainment and straight news.

So be it.

Edd Routt

About the Author

The author attended schools of journalism at Southern Methodist University and East Texas State University. His journalism background includes stints with the Associated Press Bureau in Dallas and the Dallas Morning News. He is author of **The Business of Radio Broadcasting,** TAB Books, Blue Ridge Summit, Pa., 1972, and is an instructor in station administration at Southern Methodist University. He has held virtually every middle and top management post available in the industry, from news director to general manager to president of a licensee corporation. Mr. Routt is also a former executive assistant to Gordon McLendon, president, McLendon Stations.

Introduction

The phenomenon of editorializing is one which we more often associate with newspapers than with broadcast stations. Editorializing came naturally for newspapers. For the most part, editorials serve as a means of expressing opinion and promoting a point of view. Not so with broadcast stations. Radio and television found their origin in the field of entertainment, and most people in the business still view them primarily as entertainment media. News itself is still not very thoroughly developed in the broadcasting industry, and editorializing is the younger brother of news.

Despite the fact that radio and television are still essentially entertainment media, the fact also exists that radio and television provide Americans with most of their news. During the decade of the 60s, surveys showed Americans were turning toward broadcasting and away from newspapers as their primary source for news information.

Yet, broadcast news is incomplete in many ways. News staffs are pitifully small. Often, they are composed of young people who have neither training nor experience, and who have no "senior colleagues" from whom to learn. Journalism is a stranger to too many broadcast station newsrooms. Even in the best news departments, there are seldom any true "beat reporters," men and women who are given the assignment of covering a specific agency or area and nothing else. Staffs are too small to permit beats.

Broadcast news is also incomplete, because, in most cases, there are no editorials. Editorializing is a cloak which most broadcasters find unfamiliar and uncomfortable. Of hundreds of television stations and thousands of radio stations in the United States, very few broadcast editorials. And even of those, few air editorials which truly deal with the controversial issues of the community and of the nation.

There are several reasons for this. Many station managers and owners fear the possibility—and it is a real one—of losing sponsors. The first requirement of a successful station is that it stay on the air, and the owner who is too bold and courageous may find himself speaking brave words into no microphone. This, at least, is the fear of many. However, when you look at the history of broadcast stations, there are few instances when the financial stability of a station was adversely affected by editorials. I can think of only one—a radio station in the South which was shut down because of the strong antisegregationist editorial opinions of the management. Another probable reason many radio and television stations are too timid to editorialize is the complex of federal regulations surrounding the practice. Many managers are afraid of the Fairness Doctrine and its requirements for reply in case of personal attacks and for the expression of opposing opinion.

But whatever the arguments against editorializing, they are not as compelling as those in favor of it. The editorial is the natural copestone to the straight report. It is like the period at the end of the sentence: it occupies little space, but it provides a finality and an additional meaning to what has been said before.

A few years ago, at a conference at the Columbia University Graduate School of Journalism, I was impressed by hearing former CBS News President Fred Friendly say that the job of the journalist goes beyond telling the story accurately: it includes the duty to say "Yes, but..." For example, if the mayor announces that the elimination of a city agency will save two million dollars annually, but the reporter knows, as a matter of fact, that other agencies will have to spend more money to provide the missing services, it is the reporter's responsibility to say so.

The editorial is the highest and best form of the "Yes, but..." It is also the best form of "No!" It is a way in which the licensee can offer the product of his study for the benefit of the public. It is an opportunity for him to suggest alternatives to current policies and propose new policies. It is a legitimate forum—his forum—in which he can criticize and praise public actions and public personalities. It is a means by which his voice can become an important voice in the community, for good or for bad.

With this power, of course, goes a heavy responsibility. When opinions are spoken so publicly, they should be based upon careful study, upon facts which have been checked and rechecked, and upon intelligent deliberation and discussion. Stations which editorialize should develop mechanisms which insure that these things happen. The editorial is not properly the part-time hobby of the owner.

As broadcasting grows in maturity, and becomes more and more an accepted means of serious communication rather than merely an entertainment medium, editorials will become more common than they now are. With that growth, their role in the typical newsroom will be a more integral one. Therefore, it is incumbent upon the student entering broadcast news to understand what an editorial is, its role in relationship to the news, and the techniques of writing effective editorials.

It is to that end that this book is written. Students will find here a summary of the origins and background of the broadcast editorial, the considerations involved in editorializing, the techniques of building editorials and editorial campaigns. A most valuable part of the book is the final two chapters, which contain numerous examples of how leading stations—in both large and small markets—have successfully editorialized.

I believe the day is coming when we will be able to speak of the broadcast editorial as a normal thing, not as an unusual phenomenon. But let the day never come when we stop treating it with care, and just a little awe. It is a wonderful and powerful thing, and deserving of respect.

Travis Linn, Dallas, January, 1973

Mr. Linn is executive news director, WFAA-TV, Dallas, and is vice president and president-elect of the Radio Television News Directors Association (RTND). He was graduated from Harvard University, **cum laude** in English, in 1961.

Contents

CHAPTER 1
Rhetoric in Retrospect — 13
Freedom of the Press—Step Toward Press Control—Control of Broadcasting—Decline in Divergent Papers—Need for Reforms

CHAPTER 2
The Nature of the Medium — 24
Responsiveness to Speech—Emotion Communicated—Credibility Communicated

CHAPTER 3
The Contrast of Print — 30
Techniques for Emphasis—Subjects to Be Treated

CHAPTER 4
Broadcasting: Entertainment or Communications? — 36
Financial Pressures of Broadcasting—Ratio of Entertainment to News—Influence of Audience Interest—Editorial Responsibility

CHAPTER 5
Editorializing Under the FCC — 45
Protection of First Amendment—Certification—Fear of Control—The Fairness Doctrine—The Personal Attack Rule—Sections 312 and 315, Communications Act (As Amended)—Decision to Editorialize—Meeting Reply Obligations—Libel and Slander

CHAPTER 6
Ways and Means of Editorializing — 77
A Public Affairs Department—Goals—Organization

CHAPTER 7
The Editorial — 86
Kinds of Editorials—How to Write an Editorial—Delivery—Examples of Editorials—Mailing Broadcast Editorials—Production Techniques—Editorial Campaigns

CHAPTER 8
Editorial Practices 121
WMCA, New York—Paul Harvey, ABC, Chicago—WSAU, Wasau, Wisconsin—WMAQ-TV, Chicago—KNBC, Burbank, California—KNXT, Los Angeles—WMAR, Baltimore—KOOL, Phoenix, Arizona—KIRO, Seattle—KTVU, San Francisco-Oakland—WGN, Chicago—WCBS, New York—WSB, Atlanta—WAVZ, New Haven, Connecticut

CHAPTER 9
Small- to Medium-Market Efforts 183
WNYN, Canton, Ohio—WGWR, Asheboro, North Carolina—KVGB, Great Bend, Kansas—KLPM, Minot, North Dakota

Contributors 197

Bibliography 199

Index 201

CHAPTER 1

Rhetoric in Retrospect

The power of opinion and its influence upon society has been, for almost 2500 years, an issue for debate. The earliest medium of disseminating opinion was, obviously, the rostrum, which attained a peak in power and prestige during the fifth century B.C. when the ancient Hellenic Government encouraged citizens to speak before the popular Assembly in Athens. Anyone who could legally and intellectually command an audience was allowed to articulate his thoughts and beliefs.

But the orators, especially those leaders who appeared regularly before the Assembly, were held responsible for the effect of their rhetoric. Any speaker who was suspected of offering immoral opinions or questionable advice to the people could, under the laws of the time, be impeached and prohibited from appearing before the Assembly. He was, therefore, denied the freedom to speak, because opinion, whether it reflects a mere personal prejudice or a relatively authoritative judgment, is pointless without clear amplification through effective means of dissemination. The orator who addresses an empty hall is unlikely to motivate action or inaction. The newspaper editorial writer whose material is never published and distributed cannot cure a public ill. And the broadcaster whose opinions fall to dead microphones cannot sway the public mind one way or the other.

The invention of printing gave the opiners and thought-shapers their first means of mass and enduring distribution. Printers, including such notables as Benjamin Franklin, went far beyond their trade duties of setting type and turning presses to become publishers of books, newspapers, and magazines. The freedom of the printers was surrounded by controversy from the beginning. The printed word was found to be a force for good or for evil, because books, newspapers, and magazines strongly influenced many people. In the 17th century, Dr. Samuel Johnson, English lexicographer and author, said that the freedom of printing "has produced a problem in the science of government which human understanding seems hitherto unable to solve."

FREEDOM OF THE PRESS

Throughout history, governments have sought to control the press and other means of mass communication. This has been accomplished through licensing, censorship, or monopoly. England and France, until the later 1700s, required printers to obtain formal licenses. Should the authorities find a publication unsatisfactory, the printer's license could be revoked. Russia, China, and other totalitarian governments still control printers and electronic media through censorship or outright monopoly.

In the early days of the American colonies, England exercised control over the new world press by a licensing system. The first American newspaper, **Publick Occurrences**, published in 1690, was suppressed because it did not have a license. It was an English rule of law that any criticism of the government was libelous. After 1763, the idea of a free press became part of the colonies' battle cry in their struggle for independence. Newspapers openly attacked English policy, and public opinion supported their efforts to prevent suppression.

After the colonies won their independence, the founding fathers incorporated into the Constitution of the United States much of the political philosophy of ancient Greece. They omitted, however, the intellectual and ethical restrictions upon free expression of opinion and they guaranteed a free American press which would never be subjected to governmental control. Every citizen was assured the inalienable right to express his views. There is little doubt that the exercise of the freedoms of speech and press has contributed much to the maintenance and protection of this country's free society. Thoughtful, sober men, as well as the maladroits, have always freely examined and opinionated on the day-by-day operations of a government "of, by, and for the people."

Politicians and religious leaders in this country have always taken to the "stump" or pulpit to speak their views and exhort followers to action. The veracity of their statements may or may not be questioned by the listeners, but there is no law in the United States prohibiting rhetoricians from stretching the truth or perpetrating blatant prevarications so long as such untruths are not libelous, slanderous, or designed to incite a riot. The press, too, is prohibited by law from publishing libelous statements. There are laws against obscene or indecent publications, although in recent years the courts, supported by broadening public mores, have become more lenient in interpreting them. Many governments, including that of the U.S., prohibit the publication of materials which are intended to promote violent revolution. Such **limited** control of media is desirable, even in a free society, to protect the privacy of citizens and maintain a level of order that even a democracy demands.

This freedom with limited control was not easily won. Even after the colonies gained their independence, the new government attempted to throttle the free press. The Alien and Sedition Acts of 1789 prohibited a publisher from criticizing the government. After the laws expired or were repealed under the pressure of public outrage, President Thomas Jefferson pardoned those who had been convicted under them and Congress returned the fines that had been imposed. During World War I, Congress passed several wartime censorship laws. These included the Espionage Act of 1917 and the Sedition Act of 1918. The latter, which curbed press comment on government acts, was repealed in 1921. The Espionage Act is still in force.

Nevertheless, the United States press enjoys greater freedom than that of any nation in history; and, through its freedom, it has been able to play two major roles. First, the honorary title of Fourth Estate has made it a watchdog over government at all levels. Second, the public has always been provided with divergent points of view from competing newspaper and magazine publishers. In spite of the regrettable era of yellow journalism, print media have played these roles effectively. Publishers, such as Adolph Ochs of the New York Times and Joseph Pulitzer of the New York World, served as public protectors while, at the same time, giving the public particular points of view. Ochs' credo was to "give the news impartially, without fear or favor." He separated editorial comment from news in the Times, and presented "news truthfully and free from prejudice." Pulitzer made the World "fight for progress and reform; always remain devoted to the public welfare, always remain drastically independent." Pulitzer and William Randolph Hearst were among the leaders in the era of yellow journalism when papers waged no-holds-barred battles to increase circulation. Still, such publishers deserve much credit for making news media a vital force in society. It would not be difficult to identify hundreds of newspaper publishers who have sufficient courage to vigorously exercise the press freedoms guaranteed by the First Amendment. These men have become leaders in our country, influencing public opinion to a degree at least equal to that of elected governmental officials.

Whatever qualified an individual for leadership apparently also qualified him as a commentator or "personal" journalist. A leader may be defined as an individual who is followed because of an ability to guide and control others or because he has been selected by others to be their head. There is a general tendency to think of a leader's having arrived at his position chiefly because of his talent for influencing others and for acting as a guiding force. Because leaders exist in and out of authority, the "in's" tend to suppress the "out's." Public support of a free press has unquestionably held off the "in's" who would impose government controls over those "out's" whose contrary opinions are valued by the masses.

Print media is under pressure only from readers and advertisers. Under the protection of the First Amendment, no publisher may be put out of business by a government agency even though he fails to provide the degree of fairness and public service required by that agency. One of the great tragedies in the history of America is that electronic media may not exercise the same sweep of freedoms.

STEP TOWARD PRESS CONTROL

Early in 1972 Congress passed the Federal Elections Campaign Act which, among other things, required that the press provide advertising space at regular commercial rates to candidates seeking federal office. While newspapers have always had to observe certain postal regulations and were vulnerable to assault from the Federal Trade Commission, this was the government's first move to control advertising rates. In effect, Congress told the press that every person seeking federal office must be sold advertising space on a "fair trade" basis, regardless of the individual newspaper's political leanings. It was clearly an effort to legislate morality because publishers could charge friendly candidates low rates and force unconscionably high rates on the opposition. Passage of the Act was applauded by some, while others condemned it as an infringement on the press' rights under the First Amendment. The press' right to be wrong and unfair—even though limited to a very few publications—was abolished by the Act. Conservatives or constitutionalists viewed the move as an opening gambit toward further restrictions on the press.

CONTROL OF BROADCASTING

Radio broadcasting was one of the first electronic miracles of the 20th century. Before the public, who had so vigorously defended freedom of speech and the press, could see beyond its magic and logically appraise its potential, governmental controls were imposed. Just as Greece had been fearful of the persuasive power of the trained rhetorician, just as England had imagined the printing press becoming a monster, the leaders of the free United States were at once dazzled by and afraid of the new medium. In 1922, during the infancy of radio broadcasting, the first National Radio Conference agreed that the federal government should be granted authority to control transmitting stations. Few people recognized this purely perfunctory decision as a first step in limiting the right of free speech and press. In 1927, the Federal Radio Commission was established, to be succeeded seven years later by the Federal Communications Commission.

Since then, the power of the government to manipulate expressions of opinion over the airwaves has grown to alarming proportions.

In November, 1972, Eugene C. Pulliam, publisher of the Arizona **Republic** and former owner of KTAR-AM-FM-TV, argued in a front-page editorial that "the government will take over radio and television stations in this country in a few years unless Congress takes decisive action to halt it." Pulliam said he believed the "result will be one radio and television system operated, programed—in short, completely dominated—by an elite group of Washington bureaucrats. The publisher called on newspapers to fight "the trend" since "television's hands are tied by government restrictions." By "trend," Pulliam referred to Federal Trade Commission proposals for counteradvertising, liberal proposals requiring television stations to carry two hours of children's programing daily without commercials, and strike applicants who want licenses removed from broadcasters whose "ideologies don't match up with their own."

The editorial provoked a flurry of supporting statements. FCC Chairman Dean Burch said the editorial was being studied "with pronounced interest by the broadcast industry." Burch said he personally agreed with the thesis of the message which warned against dictatorship by nonelected federal officials over what the public may and may not see on TV. Senator Paul Fannin of Arizona observed in support of Pulliam's editorial that "each year federal bureaucracies expand their power just a little more to take over functions which once were performed by individuals or through private enterprise." Fannin also said there is "a narrow-minded elitist philosophy in the Washington bureaucracy who believe they know what is best for the nation and will jam their philosophy down the people's throats whether the people like it or not." Further support came from Senator Barry Goldwater of Arizona, and Congressman William G. Bray of Indiana, to mention only two. Congressman Sam Steiger, also of Arizona, commented that the editorial addressed itself to an increasingly acute problem of bureaucratic control over intimate facets of American freedom. "The time to stop 'Big Brother' is before he has put our lives into regimented bondage." Senator Goldwater observed that Mr. Pulliam was not complaining about Arizonan FCC Chairman Burch, but rather against the liberal thinking Commissioner Nicholas Johnson, "about some of the holdover members who have suggested some very wild, far out ideas that would never work in a country like this." Johnson had lent support to broadcasters who, inadvertently or otherwise, aired obscene and offensive programs, while abhoring heavy commercial content. In the meanwhile, the role of the free press as public protector and informer has for several reasons grown less definitive.

DECLINE IN DIVERGENT PAPERS

While the press generally still functions effectively as a watchdog over government operations, the sheer economics of publishing is forcing mergers and bankruptcies, thus depriving citizens of differing points of view. In 1909, there were 689 cities in the U.S. with two or more separately owned newspapers. Sixty-two years later, there were only 36 cities left with competing daily newspapers. Because of this decline in divergent presses, the electronic media need greater, not less, freedom to state facts and comment on them without fear of retaliation by the Federal Communications Commission or of being challenged at license renewal time by those with differing points of view. In 1963, Amarillo, Texas, a city of 127,000 persons, had commonly owned morning and afternoon dailies, as do so many other cities. Thomas Martin, editorial director of KFDA-TV, Amarillo, told a House subcommittee in Washington how his station often was the sole opposition to positions taken by the local publisher.

"For example, we have a daily newspaper, which a while ago inaugurated a series of articles dealing with disarmament. And I know something about the newspaper business, and I am not reading anything into it. I am reading literally word for word. If you were to read these articles, as a fairly informed semi-intelligent human being, which I presume I am, you would be forced to conclude that a majority of the Congressmen sitting in

Washington, D.C., have deliberately passed a piece of legislation which is intended to strip this country of its defenses, its nuclear weapons, and other forms of defenses, and that in a period of 10 years this country will be defenseless before Russia."

"Now this is what the people in the city of Amarillo get via the newspaper. We do not believe it, and, by golly, we say so. As a matter of fact, we ended one of our editorials, which you have, by saying:

"'The whole proposition simply will not sell soap, even when it is wrapped in an editorial page.'"

Newspapers in the U.S. have rarely been faced with the legal necessity of being fair. Readers and advertisers have, however, forced many self-serving publishers to present the news fairly, report on all sides of controversial issues, and keep editorials on the editorial page. The broadcaster, on the other hand, is bound by law and administrative rule, as well as public pressure, to be fair and offer his facility to virtually anyone who disagrees with an editorial or particular point of view on any public issue. This country's informed public should be the best judge and censor of broadcast programing.

There have been exceptionally courageous broadcasters, such as WAVZ's Dan Kops, WMCA's R. Peter Straus, and Gordon McLendon, who became recognized community or national leaders because they broadcast strong, effective editorials. Stations WMAQ-TV and WGN-TV in Chicago, to mention only two, have performed magnificently in editorializing. But on the whole, broadcasters simply are afraid or too lethargic to voice strong editorial opinions over the air.

NEED FOR REFORM

It is not in the nature of government to voluntarily release control of any facet of a society. Once control has been achieved, the rules become more numerous and complex, and only an outraged public can stop them. It is reasonably predictable that someday broadcasters will take their case to the public and ask for a constitutional amendment that will give them the same, virtually unconditional, freedom afforded publishers. Some prominent licensees believe stations are already covered by the First Amendment and prefer to fight for recognition of this belief by government leaders. It was fallacious in those experimental days for government to assume that airways belonged in the public domain and that it should control anyone choosing to use them. It is more fallacious today.

Control advocates argue that broadcasting is a public utility and, therefore, should be controlled. Every argument supporting more controls over broadcasting is based upon the original and illogical assumption that government had a right to exercise such control. Newspapers and magazines are sold on public streets; they are delivered to homes on public streets, and they are given special postal rates when publishers deliver by mail. Many industries use the public domain for commercial purposes, but they are not licensed, hobbled, and harrassed by a government administration agency. Ayn Rand, writing in the April, 1964 issue of "The Objectivist Newsletter" said, "There is no difference in principle between the ownership of land and the ownership of airways."

The U.S. over the years has supported Radio Free Europe (RFE), thus enabling that huge electronic medium to provide millions of people behind the iron curtain with truths not available through communist-controlled radio stations. Even the U.S. Government would be indignant if Russia or some other communistic nation demanded equal time on RFE. The Voice of America facility makes similar contributions to the philosophy of truth as we see it. Yet, should the United Nations attempt to legislate controls over such stations, every politician and government official in the country would leap forward with cries of "tyranny" and "suppression." Some would wave the flag of freedom with one hand, while holding domestic U.S broadcasting's head under water with the other.

Broadcasters, politicians, liberals, conservatives, and extremists of every creed have proposed solutions to the inequities. Each bases his interpretation of "public interest" and "fairness" upon his own particular point of view and favorite philosophy. The arguments range from the capitalistic philosophy of Ayn Rand to the iron-fisted tirades of Nicholas Johnson.

"With a limited supply and a growing demand," Miss Rand argues, "competition would have driven the market value of a radio (and later, TV) station so high that only the most competent men could have afforded to buy it or to keep it; a man unable to make a profit could not long afford to waste so valuable a property." Miss Rand assumed that if a man can afford to buy a station, he is, therefore, competent. Likewise, she argues, any man who can make a profit from a station is surely a competent man. "Competency," by her definition, should be the criterion for "fairness." The only solution at so late a date, she proposes, is "to sell all radio and television frequencies to the highest bidders, by an objectively defined, open, impartial process." How such a solution could be "impartial" to current station owners who have invested money and resources in their operations is not explained.

Syndicated columnist, Carl Rowan, exhibits some ambivalence in his view. He accepts, from his own position as a spokesman for the printed media, the concept that television and radio have a responsibility to air all sides of controversy. Without even a blush, he proclaims, "The public does have a greater claim on TV (and radio) than on newspapers and magazines because the airwaves are limited and are the property of all the people." The argument that the airwaves are limited is one of the most inane offered. In 1972, there were over 7000 broadcast facilities in the U.S. compared to some 1700 daily newspapers. The limitations of the broadcast spectrum prevent fewer people from operating stations than do the economic factors of our society. Typically, Rowan's only quarrel is with the politicians. "The people are sure to suffer," he insists, "if they swallow the notion that the only way to get 'fairness' is to have politicians decree it. When politicians start jockeying for advantage, they can't agree on the color of the sky, but each one knows an unfair, too powerful journalist: one who has just hurt him. Politicians are blinded by an insatiable thirst for survival, and 'fairness' to them is one-dimensional. Government ought never be the judge of the 'fairness' of TV or any other part of the press."

Although broadcasters in the United States should be as free as printers to practice editorial rhetoric, the simple fact is, they are not. The student and the rising young broadcaster must, therefore, learn the art and practice it within the framework of existing laws and rules. They should, at the same time, learn to believe that if broadcasting is ever to be completely and unconditionally free, the practitioners must be responsible, community-conscious individuals who will voluntarily stamp upon the walls of their stations such words as fairness, public service, progress, and reform.

CHAPTER 2

The Nature of the Medium

The living word, even though it may be enunciated from a printed text, has an indefinite and perhaps immeasurable capability of moving persons to act for or against a stated fact or situation. A word or idea expressed without conviction or emotion may have no more effect upon the hearer than the same communication in a newspaper or magazine. The spoken word, therefore, may be dramatic only if the deliverer injects drama into its enunciation. Eighteenth-century writer John Ward pointed out that bare conviction is not sufficient to excite many people to action. John Priestley, the English author, looked upon emotion as an "energizer and expediter of conduct."

Broadcasting, particularly television and to a slightly lesser extent modern radio, is a medium through which speakers may employ every known rhetorical maneuver in their efforts to move others to action. Different techniques work for different broadcasters, depending upon the audience spoken to or the subject matter covered.

To some recipients, a word is a word is a word when it is simply printed on paper. It conveys no meaning until it is spoken. Even then, unless the word is spoken dramatically, it still has no meaning. In an unlikely but illustrative situation, a clerk hands a typed message to the store manager:

"There is a fire in the basement."

The busy manager reads the memo, does not relate the message to the problems he is considering at the moment, and thus is not moved to action.

Another clerk, not wishing to create a panic, approaches the manager and says, quietly, "There is a fire in the basement." The import of the communication still has not moved the manager to action.

A stockboy, feeling the heat of the fire, dashes flush-faced to the manager's desk and, waving his arms wildly, shouts, "THERE'S A FIRE IN THE BASEMENT!" The person not moved by this dramatic presentation of the facts perhaps cannot be moved by any sort of communication.

RESPONSIVENESS TO SPEECH

Consider the local editorial in yesterday's newspaper. It is being discussed by members of a car pool.

JOHN: How about that editorial in yesterday's paper!

BILL: What editorial?

JOHN: The one about the new city hall.

BILL: Oh, yeah. So what? So those politicians down there are going to build themselves a new nest. So what else is new?

JOHN: You seem pretty unconcerned, Bill.

BILL: So?

JOHN: So, darn it, Bill...IF THEY SUCCEED IT'LL RAISE YOUR TAXES BY 25 PERCENT!!!

BILL: You're kidding!

JOHN: No. I thought you **read** the editorial!

BILL: I did read it. But I guess it didn't register.

SAM: Same with me, fellows. I read the editorial, but the implications didn't register with me until I heard a similar editorial last night on the radio.

JOHN: You guys. Neither of you gets a picture from reading. Bill didn't get the import of the editorial until I **told** him about

25

it. And Sam didn't either, until he **heard** about it on the radio. You guys are "ear" oriented; you don't get the message until someone **speaks** it to you.

H. V. Kaltenborn, one of radio's earliest commentators, believed the average citizen "is much more **responsive** to what he hears than to what he reads." He said, "There can be no question about the superior persuasive power of speech." While Kaltenborn's assertion is undoubtedly true, there are other persons who believe only what they read in print. The responsiveness referred to by Kaltenborn may result **only** when the communicated message is dramatized, as when the stockboy accompanied his "THERE'S A FIRE IN THE BASEMENT!" with waving arms, strident voice, and red face. Response, therefore, frequently results from an emotional reaction rather than a mental assessment of the information received. How often we say, "He acted before he thought," or, "I did it without thinking." These undoubtedly are **emotional responses** to information communicated orally. To some people, if the information is printed, it is credible, regardless of the author and the publication. If the same material is **spoken** (or broadcast), it is credible only if the listener can personally vouch for the character and integrity of the speaker.

EMOTION COMMUNICATED

Many politicians are masters at spoken rhetoric and have throughout the ages been able to persuade audiences of their personal credibility through speech delivery methods as opposed to discoursing on sound ideas. Plato felt that orators could deal successfully in words without knowledge. Extemporaneous speakers also were held in contempt in Archibald Philip Primrose's "Life of Pitt," in 1891. He wrote: "Few speeches which have produced an electrical effect on an audience can bear the colorless photography of a printed record." Al Kelly, noted humorist and double-talk artist, once imitated a political speech with a highly emotional, arm-waving harangue in which he spoke only letters from the alphabet. It took his audience in Dallas fully one minute to realize that Kelly was only emoting, that he was not making an effort to convey a single idea.

Rhetoricians define two primary styles of speaking or adding dramatic effect to spoken words. "Atticism" is a simple, restrained style that perhaps would be used by a very correct Englishman. "Asianism," on the other hand, might be used to describe the manner employed by Huey Long, one time governor of Louisiana. Long's style was florid, luxuriant in southern Louisiana idioms, and often bombastic. Long and his constituents would have been unimpressed by the soft-spoken, understating Englishman. The Englishman doubtlessly would have been appalled by Long's shouting, flamboyant, arm-waving style.

The voice itself often communicates, even though the hearer may not understand the words being spoken. Al Kelly's harangue is one example, but there are other appropriate ones. When the song "Dominique" was first recorded by The Singing Nun, the words were in French. The words were not important, obviously, because the tune became an overnight hit in America. The singer's emotional outpouring said all that needed to be said. Many of the world's great operas are performed in tongues foreign to many members of the audiences, but are appreciated and "felt" no less because of this gap. At a bullfight in Mexico, Portugal, or Spain, what monolingual American doesn't thrill to the cries of "Ole!" from the Spanish-speaking crowds?

When Franklin Roosevelt, one of the first U.S. Presidents to make effective use of radio, conducted his Fireside Chats, a listener could sense the nation's trouble and the President's concern by his "mood" or the "dramatic delivery" of his messages without ever really understanding the strict meaning of his words. Roosevelt's style was not bombastic; it was, indeed, a combination of the attic and asian techniques. The President employed the restrained simplicity of the attic style as well as the emotionalism of the asian technique. When Roosevelt talked of America's involvement in World War II, the masses listened. And they listened because the President was able to convey emotionalism and credibility in one and the same voice.

CREDIBILITY COMMUNICATED

The nation listened in awesome reverence when, on December 8, 1941, President Roosevelt intoned:

"Yesterday, December 7, 1941—a date which will live in infamy—the United States of America was suddenly and deliberately attacked by naval and air forces of the Empire of Japan."

This was part of Roosevelt's famous "War Message to Congress," which was broadcast on radio nationwide and called upon Congress to declare a state of war. Roosevelt used radio to calm and fortify a nation outraged by the sneak Japanese attack. His on-the-air rhetoric was matched only by that of Britain's Prime Minister, Winston Churchill, and was in direct contrast to the wild, maniacal tirades of Germany's Adolph Hitler and Italy's Benito Mussolini.

Roosevelt's Fireside Chats were the administration's chief vehicle for synergizing American resources to make an effective entry into World War II. In his Fireside Chat of February 23, 1942, the President said: "Never before have we had so little time in which to do so much."

Churchill, about two years earlier, had said: "Never in the field of human conflict was so much owed by so many to so few."

Churchill, too, made dramatic and effective use of his rhetorical ability on radio. Adult Americans of the time heard via shortwave radio a determined Churchill say:

"We shall defend every village, every town, and every city. The vast mass of London itself, fought street by street, could easily devour an entire hostile army; and we would rather see London laid in ruins and ashes than that it should be tamely and abjectly enslaved."

The **spoken** word may be delivered mechanically as with the court bailiff's, "Hear Ye! This court is now in session, the Honorable So-and-So presiding," or with deep emotion and feeling as in Roosevelt's and Churchill's historical utterances. The works of Shakespeare may serve as an excellent example of how dramatically spoken words can bring cold type to life. To many, to read Shakespeare is a nightmare of alien passages and words that speak nothing. But when Richard Burton interprets **Hamlet,** Shakespeare's ideas assume unbelievably human shapes and forms.

Perhaps Marshall McLuhan's "The Medium is the Message" concept will be absolved of any truth when man grasps or regrasps his talent for the oral expression of well conceived ideas. Orations may be meaningless, as demonstrated by comedian Al Kelly. But they may be worthy of print and enduring consideration as illustrated by Roosevelt and Churchill.

CHAPTER 3

The Contrast of Print

British essayist and critic William Hazlitt described the difference between writing and extemporary or impromptu speaking in terms of "time." He exhibited contempt for the "popular speaker" and a deep respect for the writer. "The chief requisite (for the speaker) appears to be quickness and facility of perception," he wrote, "and for writing, patience of soul, and a power increasing with the difficulties it has to master." Of the "popular speaker," Hazlitt said he is "like a vulgar actor off the stage. Take away his cue, and he has nothing to say for himself." Hazlitt doubted that the speaker could ever move beyond the commonplace. "If he does, he gets beyond his hearers," he suggested, adding, "The most successful speakers have not been the best scholars or the finest writers. Those speeches that told best **at the time**, are now readable."

In dealing with the differences between broadcast and print editorials, one must consider the spans that separate writing from speaking, although both fall under the definition of contemporary rhetoric. In both cases, the material is written. The chief difference is in **delivery** of the material to the masses.

Doubtlessly, there are many speakers who should never be on the rostrum. Even with delicately and carefully prepared texts, they do not communicate. In contrast, there are mental midgets whose ability to interpret someone else's editorial material makes them appear brilliant. Some radio and TV on-the-air newsmen are simply readers who could not be trusted to speak extemporaneously on the air and whose communication talents stop just this side of lucid thought. Consider the on-the-air character in The Mary Tyler Moore Show on (CBS) television. In this excellent example, "Ted," as he is known, is the news department's dummy; all the brains are supplied by the editor and his writers. "Ted" merely mouths the intelligence developed by the editorial staff.

Broadcasting is different from reading. Broadcasting employs, for communication purposes, the human voice with its infinite capacity to provoke laughter, hate, fear, compassion, and to stimulate and foment action by the hearers. This conclusion does not mean to imply that thoughts expressed in writing (and perceived by the eye) cannot motivate. To the contrary, the world's literature attests to the capacity of print to activate every human emotion and stimulate every human reaction. There will always be those who believe everything they read, and regard as hearsay everything they hear. Further, there will always be others who simply cannot understand what they read and, therefore, will react only to what they hear. Therefore, it may be impossible to determine whether a broadcast editorial or a newspaper editorial has the greater impact upon the masses. Each side of the controversy can establish "proof" that one is better than the other, much as the palmist can "prove" by using only positive cases that she indeed can read one's future and past by interpreting the lines in the palm.

TECHNIQUES FOR EMPHASIS

In terms of delivery, the newspaper is not without its attention-getting devices. While the broadcast editorial makes full use of the capabilities of the human voice, the printed editorial employs bold-face type, thick, black borders, special headlines and body type, extra large body type, and other typographical innovations designed to get and hold the attention of the reader. In issuing a run-of-the-mill editorial, neither medium has resorted extensively to the use of pictures (in the case of newspapers) or music and other sound effects (in the case of radio and television stations).

Surveys indicate that the editorial page of the newspaper is the least read of the entire paper. The same must be true of broadcast editorials and certainly is true of most "opinion" or "commentary" shows. Sol Taishoff, chairman and editor of Broadcasting, told the Radio and Television News Directors Association in 1967 that "most broadcast editorializing is dull. Too many broadcast editorialists have merely adapted the technique of the print editorial. They face the microphone and camera with somber voice and stern expression and read from the gospel of the moment. And their presentation and message are as gray as the columns of inert type on the average American newspaper's editorial page. I claim the license to make these statements because I have in my time filled a good many gray columns of type myself, and I do not think they deserve to be the model for broadcast editorialists who have at their command an infinite range of sounds and pictures."

Notable exceptions to Taishoff's generally correct indictment may be found in the sections of this text dealing with WMAQ-TV and WGN-TV's production techniques. Dull presentations result from the average broadcaster's reluctance to provoke meaningful community reaction to editorials. Often, editorials are aired simply because they help the licensee fulfill his public affairs commitment to the FCC. At other times, the licensee and his staff simply do not have the imagination required to produce provocative editorials. Such indolence can result only from the licensee's failure to understand any purpose beyond making a substantial return on his investment.

In his address to RTNDA, Taishoff quoted Senator Phil Hart of Michigan as saying broadcast editorials would be more effective if they borrowed the creative techniques of the better broadcast commercials. Taishoff is one of the broadcast industry's most respected and outspoken critics.

SUBJECTS TO BE TREATED

Any effort to compare broadcast and print editorials should consider the real or imagined controls under which the broadcaster must prepare and air his exhortations. As considered earlier, it is relatively easy for the knowing and fair-minded licensee to effectively editorialize without suffering more than some "extra duty" in handling the paperwork that may result from complaints to the FCC and from the Fairness

Doctrine requirement that the licensee affirmatively seek opposing points of view. The licensee who does not take an intelligent overview of his role and accompanying rules will indeed risk his license and right to continue operating. The licensee who uses his facility to promote his private well-being and that of his friends and cronies endangers not only his property but also the right of stations everywhere to play a significant role in community leadership.

Taishoff, in the same speech, challenged broadcasters to deal with more controversial subjects in their editorials. "An enlivening of technique will not in itself turn the broadcast editorial into the mover and shaker of the audience it reaches. The content of the message must be at least as sharp as the method of message delivery (emphasis mine). A defense of motherhood or the flag does not really lend itself to terribly imaginative production.

"In recent years, there has been a noticeable trend toward the exploration of more controversial subjects. Indeed, one out of 10 stations has gone so far as to endorse political candidates, according to a NAB (National Association of Broadcasters) survey. But the ventures into really nitty gritty issues are more the exception than the rule. It is a rare editorial that endorses an unpopular cause, however just.

"Why should this be so? Well, some of my best friends are station managers, and I am, therefore, in a position to detect here and there a congenital disinclination to rock the boat. I daresay some of you may have heard reports of managers who think it fiscally and socially imprudent to disturb the reigning preconceptions of the locker room.

"But conservative management is neither so numerous nor so timid as to deserve the principal blame for the infrequency of gutsy editorializing. The real culprit is that regulatory monstrosity of FCC creation, the Fairness Doctrine. In the NAB survey that I mentioned, nearly 60 percent of all station managers asserted that the Fairness Doctrine had inhibited their treatment of controversial subjects. Surely there is no working newsman of any significant experience in radio or television who has not at some time found his editorial judgments affected by the knowledge that the FCC stands

33

ready to receive and magnify almost any asinine grievance that a news report or editorial may arouse."

Taishoff's summary of broadcasters' fears regarding editorializing were stated elsewhere in 1963 by other broadcasters. At a congressional hearing in Washington, D.C., Jesse Holmes, WRAL-TV, Raleigh, N.C., proclaimed that "the trouble with limitations and restraint is that they tend to discourage open expressions. Many a radio or television station operator would rather not bother with an expensive, time-consuming responsibility if it is likely to cause them trouble—and certainly not if he entertains the idea that he may lose his right to operate."

Leon Goldstein, representing the American Civil Liberties Union, at the same hearing, declared, "The broadcaster has always been afraid of congressional reprisal for the airing of opinions contrary to officeholders and office seekers. For that reason, perhaps, too many broadcasters still editorialize on behalf of green grass and motherhood, rather than on real issues."

Contrast these views and attitudes with those of the print world. Everett T. Rattray, editor of **The East Hampton Star** (New York State), said that "a newspaper's job, according to the oldtimers, is to print the news and raise hell. It is my belief that any newspaper that reports accurately the doings of local government over a period of years is bound to make that government a better one, and make its area a better place in which to live."

While broadcasting has three cogent objections to editorializing (governmental reprisal, public disdain, and economics), newspapers, under the strong and hopefully secure First Amendment, are faced only with the possibility of public disdain and the dollar problem. Rattray, in his essay written for **The Responsibility of the Press**, edited by Gerald Gross and published by Fleet Publishing Company, New York, emphasized the social and economic aspects of editorializing in the newspaper. "There is a big if involved, however. This reporting can only be done if the paper survives. Survival means money from advertising, unless the publisher is a multimillionaire with a yearning for a tax loss. Can there be survival in the face of community disapproval, including the dislike of most of the advertisers?

"....even the most idealistic editor will rarely find himself at odds with the majority of his readers at once. A good paper will eventually offend them all, but most likely do it a few at a time. Survival ought to be possible."

Some newspapers, for reasons of laziness, ineptitude, fear of public denial, or economic hardship also are guilty of editorially favoring motherhood and green grass. Rattray cites the example of a colleague:

"The (newspaper) owner is easily sickened by a rocking boat, so the three or four editorials a year are confined to deploring communism, drunken driving, or riding bicycles on the sidewalk.

"Of the American weeklies printing editorials regularly, and probably a minority of them do, a good many devote much of their comment to congratulations to the oldest citizen on her birthday, the Lions Club on their barbecue, or the Girl Scouts on their cookies. Taking into our accounting these weeklies regularly using canned editorials about the sacred right to work, the American Way of Life, and the need for more highways, it would appear that editorials interpreting local events and commenting upon them in an intelligent and honest fashion occupy but a small portion of each Thursday's newsprint across the nation.

"Why should this surprise anyone? This situation is no better with the dailies. Newspapers are newspapers, and their responsibility is to print the news and raise hell. Most of them, weekly and daily, are not performing this function very well."

Each medium has its heroes, its abstainers, and its Milquetoasts—and doubtless it will always be that way. There are licensees who will never recognize broadcasting as a means of doing anything other than entertaining and making a living. And there are publishers who feel that objective reporting of the news adequately fulfills the role of print journalism. Some cannot lead and, therefore, will not lead. This task, as always, falls to the hell-raising strong.

CHAPTER 4
Broadcasting: Entertainment or Communications?

There has never been a serious debate about the role of the newspaper in society. Print professionals agreed long ago that their chief commodity is news. Critics have doubted that the newspaper consistently performs its role properly or as effectively as possible, but no one has ever called the newspaper anything more or less than a purveyor of news, commentary, and opinion.

Newspapers, of course, attempt to provide literary and graphic entertainment. And it would be difficult to prove that they haven't been entertaining. Lurid, as well as family oriented, comic strips have been standard newspaper fare for years. Pundits such as Art Buchwald, Virginia Payette, and Earl Wilson have provoked chortles and guffaws in readers for a long time. Newspapers can provide humor, but essentially they communicate the news in writing.

Radio and television haven't been so fortunate in exhibiting a positive, definitive form. CBS commentator Eric Sevareid described television as partially show business and partially entertainment. Sevareid, making the statement in an interview with Louis M. Lyons, curator of the Nieman Fellowships at Harvard, agreed that newspapers attempt to entertain, "but not quite to the same extent. People normally do not sit down in front of the television set in the same frame of mind in which they pick up a newspaper or magazine. This is why television commercials irritate, and newspaper (advertisements) do not."

Lyons, in the same discussion, credited sponsors with deciding whether people want "news or entertainment, controversy or comics." And this, Lyons said, "has seriously complicated the problem of getting news and information through what is chiefly a medium of entertainment."

The government-owned British and Canadian broadcasting systems are examples of how broadcasting can concentrate on public affairs and esthetic programing designed to develop a more sophisticated society. In England, there is no competition from commercial operators who must attract substantial mass audiences in order to survive. In late 1972, however, the idea of commercial stations was being entertained by the English parliament. In Canada, private broadcasting does exist and in no case studied was there a government-owned facility more popular with listeners than privately owned ones. Government-owned stations in both countries too often produce boring public information and news programs by bored personnel. It seems to be the nature of government-financed operators to perform perfunctorily rather than esthetically or creatively.

While newspapers have chiefly confined hard news to the news columns, whether written objectively or subjectively, and humor and opinion to other sections of the paper, radio and television stations often are constrained to mix the news with humor. The newspaper will often "box" a humorous item on the front page. It is humor, but it is clearly separate from other stories on the same page. In broadcasting, humor often is presented in bad taste when it follows or precedes a story involving human tragedy.

During the early 1970s, many television stations were establishing entertainment news formats, with wisecracks and chit-chat interspersed between news items. Why not present news shows, as opposed to news broadcasts? CBS News anchor man, Walter Cronkite, said the technique is "like putting the comics on the front page of the newspaper." Cronkite predicted that if the entertainment news format ever hit the national networks, "it will mean the death of television news."

The CBS veteran suggested "if we had time we could compartmentalize comedy. But to interlace the entire newscast with it is abominable. It tears down everything the Edward R. Murrows have built up, and destroys the integrity and honesty of television news."

Cronkite believes that neither the broadcast nor print medium is doing the best job possible in presenting the news.

"I have said for many years that if most people are getting all their news from television, then they are inadequately informed. The trouble is, that the newspapers aren't doing their job either. Many papers, now in a monopoly situation, are not monitored by competition."

FINANCIAL PRESSURES OF BROADCASTING

Fred Friendly, one-time president of CBS News, wrote a tortured letter of resignation to his bosses at CBS when his decision to carry certain news programing was overruled. Friendly's letter has become a classic example of the chasm that often exists between broadcast programers and broadcast journalists. It stated:

"The concept of an autonomous news organization responsible only to the chairman and the president was not a creation of mine. It is a concept almost as old as CBS News, and is a tradition nurtured by the Ed Klaubers, the Ed Murrows, the Paul Whites, and rigidly enforced by both of you..."

"My departure is a matter of conscience. At the end of the day it is the viewer and the listener who have the biggest stake in all this. Perhaps my action will be understood by them. I know it will be understood by my colleagues in news and I know Ed Murrow would have understood. A speech he delivered to the RTND in 1958 spelled it all out:

'One of the basic troubles with radio and television news is that both instruments have grown up as an incompatible combination of show business, advertising, and news. Each of the three is a rather bizarre and demanding profession. And when you get all three under one roof, the dust never settles. The top management of the networks, with a few notable exceptions, has been trained in advertising, research, sales, or show business. But, by the nature of the corporate structure, they also make the final and crucial decisions having to do with news and public affairs.

'Frequently, they have neither the time nor the competence to do that. It is not easy for the same small group of men to decide whether to buy a new station for millions of dollars, build a new building, alter the rate card, buy a new western, sell a soap opera, decide what defensive line to take in connection with the latest congressional inquiry, how much money to spend on promoting a new program, what additions or deletions should be made in the existing covey or clutch of vice presidents, and at the same time—frequently on the same long day—to give mature, thoughtful consideration to the manifold problems that confront those who are charged with the responsibility for news and public affairs.'

Murrow went on to say:

'Upon occasion, economics and editorial judgment are in conflict. And there is no law which says that dollars will be defeated by duty. Not so long ago, the President of the United States delivered a television address to the nation. He was discoursing on the possibility or probability of war between this nation and the Soviet Union and Communist China—a reasonably compelling subject. Two networks—CBS and NBC—delayed that broadcast for an hour and 15 minutes. If this decision was dictated by anything other than financial reasons, the networks didn't deign to explain those reasons. That hour-and-15-minute delay, by the way, is about twice the time required for an ICBM to travel from the Soviet Union to major targets in the United States. IT IS DIFFICULT TO BELIEVE THAT THIS DECISION WAS MADE BY MEN WHO LOVE, RESPECT, AND UNDERSTAND NEWS.

'There is no suggestion here that networks or individual stations should operate as philanthropies. I can find nothing in the Bill of Rights or the Communications Act which says that they must increase their net profits each year, lest the republic collapse.'''

Friendly resigned from CBS because he was overruled on his decision to carry coverage of the hearings on the Viet Nam War before the Senate Foreign Relations Committee. This happened in February, 1966. Instead of carrying the hearings, the network carried what Friendly called a "fifth rerun of Lucy, followed by an eighth rerun of The Real McCoys." The order to kill the scheduled broadcast of the hearings came from Jack Schneider, whom Friendly quoted as saying, "The housewife isn't interested (in the hearings)."

RATIO OF ENTERTAINMENT TO NEWS

Most broadcast facilities have struggled from the beginning to determine a viable ratio of entertainment to news. It is a general practice among major market stations at least to make the news department answerable to top management instead of to program directors. The three major television networks maintain strict separation between public affairs, news, and entertainment programing. Most news directors at station level receive pay and authority equal to that of program managers or directors. These, among other developments, have added stature to broadcast journalism.

While radio and television have the obvious capacity to inform and entertain, the journalistic aspect of the medium has been slow in developing. Maturing of the medium as a purveyor of news has been retarded by (1) the unavailability of properly trained personnel; (2) late arriving technology, and (3) the essential character of the individuals who applied for and received licenses to operate broadcast facilities.

The businessman who builds a newspaper knows precisely how he will operate if he is to be successful. He must cover the news and sell enough advertising to pay operating expenses, retire debt, and provide a return on his investment. The publisher (printer, in fact) can augment his income through job printing and circulation. Herein lies the broadcaster's most frustrating problem. If he had only **news** to deliver, the problem of a commodity could be easily resolved. But U.S. commercial broadcast properties are geared to be **entertaining** as well as **informative.** So? How much news, how much entertainment? The broadcaster may program an all-news format if he can afford this most expensive of all formulas. In alternative, he must provide entertainment and then enter a guessing game as to how much nonentertainment programing (news, public affairs, and other) the FCC will require or expect him to place on his schedule. The publisher publishes information and sells space to advertisers. The broadcaster's problem obviously is far more complicated.

INFLUENCE OF AUDIENCE INTEREST

The publisher can prove through audit his circulation into his community's homes. He cannot prove conclusively that subscribers read his paper, but he logically assumes that if a family pays for the paper it certainly will read it. The Daniel Starch Company surveyed newspaper readership and indicated that every ad is not understood nor even read by every member of the family. If no one read anything in the paper, the publisher still would have a good argument to sell advertising, based solely upon circulation or papers delivered. This, of course, is not true with the broadcaster. He cannot prove conclusively that his signal is heard in a particular number of homes. He can only speculate and base his arguments on "samplings" of homes within his coverage area. These audience estimates—and the FTC policy requires that survey fallacies be published when the estimates are published—only indicate how many persons **may** be listening or viewing. The publisher prints and distributes his newspaper. Aside from a few typographical innovations, that's it. He can honestly and honorably do little more to encourage citizens to buy his commodity. The broadcaster has an infinitely wider range in the selection of material to attract listeners and viewers. He can entertain!

In the Lyons-Sevareid interview, Lyons credited advertisers with believing the public is more interested in entertainment—the whodunit and western—than in good news reporting. Sevareid, however, said he felt commercial interests had always underestimated the public interest in information.

There are some who urge that broadcasting and newspapers stick to the facts in handling news. Roscoe Drummond, one time Washington correspondent for the Christian Science Monitor, said...by and large the news stories do not, and I think cannot, alone present an intelligible picture of events. If the picture is to be intelligible, what happened yesterday has to be fitted in with what happened last week and long before that, and with what could happen, and what may happen tomorrow and in the future."

Felix R. McKnight, when he was managing editor of **The Dallas Morning News**, said,...people are comment-hungry (witness the rise of radio and TV commentators)...world problems are so complex that the reader, hurried and confused, needs a page which interprets what's happening."

Gordon McLendon, president of McLendon Stations, designed his editorials to "teach and move to action." He felt there was "no way for listeners to understand important news if the important actions of government aren't explained by editorials."

EDITORIAL RESPONSIBILITY

Fred Fuller Shedd, one time editor of the **Philadelphia Evening Bulletin**, said in 1931: "The editorial writer must fight the people's battles." He advised newspapers to "take the public's case, if it has one—the big interests can hire their own lawyers. There is an implied contract that the newspaper shall serve the public interest."

The Bergen Evening Record, Hackensack, N.J., said, "It's a case of taking up the fight for many a Joe who is unable to express himself." The **St. Louis Post-Dispatch**, in 1947, said, "the editorial page can defend the interest of the people against corrupt and incompetent public officials." Herman Ullstein, writing **The Rise and Fall of the House of Ullstein**, commented,"...the moment they start printing nothing but news—abandoning comment and criticism—they lose half their importance, and become shadows of their former selves."

Alan Barth, editorial writer for the **Washington Post** in 1952, said, "The paramount function of the press in the American social system is censorship of the government. It was primarily in order to enable it to fulfill this function that the founders of the republic insisted upon adding to the constitution as its first amendment—and as the first article in its Bill of Rights—a flat, absolute prohibition against any government regulation of the press. The idea that the press ought to serve as a censor of the government was explicitly stated by Thomas Jefferson who said (in a letter to George

Washington in 1792) 'No government ought to be without censors, and while the press is free, no one will.' "

Clearly, the news divisions of the great networks and the news departments of agressive stations want more time in the broadcast day to be devoted to the presentation of news and information.

Norman E. Isaacs, writing in **The Responsibility of the Press,** said that "Radio revolutionized journalism. Radio is a medium of instantaneous transmission. Radio helped kill the extra. One doesn't want an extra with three paragraphs of bulletin material, already heard on every radio station in the nation. What the reader wants from his newspaper is the complete story. He doesn't want opinion. He wants interpretation. He has a right to his own opinions."

Isaacs described a good newspaper as one that is honest, just, courageous, and clean; one that is growing, leads, has a conscience, and good manners. He said there are "more than just a handful of such good newspapers in this land. And not all are big papers. William Allen White proved that they didn't have to be big to be good."

Robert Sarnoff, son of broadcast pioneer David Sarnoff, made the following statements in early 1960:

1. Broadcasting, as a mass medium, best serves the public interest through programing which meets the desires and interest of the majority of people.

2. Broadcasting assumes a secondary function of programing for minority tastes and interests and, by doing so, offers the majority continuing opportunity to absorb new interest.

3. Broadcasting's responsibility to the public is harmonious with its responsibility to advertisers, for the more effectively it serves the public, the greater value it offers advertisers.

4. Broadcasting depends on public acceptance of its programs in competition with all other forms of entertainment and information and can best serve the public through the free play of competition, and with a minimum of government regulation.

5. Broadcasting, as the nation's greatest unifying communications force in peace or war, is entitled to the standing and privileges of other free communication media.

Mr. Sarnoff's father argued in 1916 that radio ought to be endowed by government, thus taking it out of the competitive area his son supported some 40 years later.

Regarding item 4 in the NBC Board Chairman's dissertation, the Report of the Commission on Freedom of the Press recommended that the constitutional "guarantees of the freedom of the press be recognized as including the radio and motion pictures." First published in 1947, the report was signed by such august members as Archibald MacLeish and Arthur M. Schlesinger.

Henry Luce, publisher of **Time, Life,** and **Fortune** magazines, was so upset by some aspects of the Commission on Freedom of the Press that he withdrew his financial support. Luce did not believe in objective reporting. He said, "Time will not allow the stuffed dummy of impartiality to stand in the way of telling the truth as it sees it." The commission's report said in part:

"The first requirement is that the media should be accurate. They should not lie...Giant units (of the press) can and should assume the duty of publishing significant ideas contrary to their own...The press ought to identify the sources of its facts, opinion, and arguments so that the reader...can judge them..."

It is apparent that many broadcasters still don't know what they really are, or what their fundamental goals in the medium are or should be. Broadcasting can admirably meet both challenges—that of entertainment for mass audiences and that of intelligence (news, editorials, commentaries, etc.) for those citizens who desire it. Some broadcasters say, "Money is the name of the game!" Indications are that in the future the public and government will insist that the sentence read, "Money and responsibility are the names of the game!"

CHAPTER 5

Editorializing Under the FCC

There is no law or FCC rule, regulation, or policy that prohibits a licensee from broadcasting editorials. Unlike his kinsman with an unlicensed press, however, the broadcaster must chart his editorial path carefully, lest he run afoul of laws and regulations that become effective after the editorial has been aired.

The most often met policy is the Federal Communications Commission's Fairness Doctrine. Where printers have always had the option to be unfair or biased, if it pleased them, broadcasters have no such choice. The Fairness Doctrine, essentially an FCC policy, requires that if a licensee expresses an editorial point of view on any controversial subject of public interest, he must make an affirmative effort to procure and put on the air opposing points of view. If the broadcaster doesn't make the affirmative effort, or, at least, yield to opponents who hear the editorial and demand time to express differing ideas, he may be subjected to an FCC hearing and a challenge to his license when next that license is up for renewal.

The same principle applies when someone other than the licensee voices a point of view over the licensee's station. Air time must be provided for those with differing points of view. The licensee may decide upon a responsible spokesman and he may choose the form in which other opinions are given. The licensee may not deny time to the opposition simply because the opposition's point of view is unpopular. Robert Harold Scott of Palo Alto, California, petitioned the FCC in 1945, requesting revocation of the licenses of radio stations KQW, KPO, and KFRC (all California) on grounds the stations refused him time to speak on atheism. Scott argued that since the stations permitted the broadcast of religious programs, he

45

was entitled to time for antireligious talks. The stations had denied Scott time on grounds that the broadcasting of atheistic talks would not be in the public interest. The Commission denied Scott's petition, but issued, in essence, the following statement:

> Stations cannot make time available for all possible points of view. But this fact cannot serve as a basis for denying time to those holding unpopular points of view.

The Commission thus warned licensees not to use its decision in the Scott case as precedent for future decisions involving public controversial issues.

In another Fairness case, the Commission voted 6-0 against renewing the licenses for Dr. Carl McIntire's WXUR-AM-FM stations in Media, Pennsylvania. The decision was upheld by the U.S. Court of Appeals in Washington, D.C. The Fairness Doctrine was one of three issues involved, and it was based largely on the stations' broadcast of a number of commentary programs, including the **20th Century Reformation Hour,** regarded by some as right wing. Complainants in the case argued that such programs were not balanced by other programs expressing different points of view. The stations argued that balance was achieved through news programs, interview shows, and call-in shows. The Commission rejected the stations' showing as inadequate. Judge Edward Tamm, in a 92-page opinion, noted that the ultimate test in determining whether a broadcaster had met his fairness obligations is "reasonableness." He also noted that another court has held that fairness only requires a good-faith effort on the part of the broadcaster (Broadcasting, Oct. 2, 1972).

The licensee who assiduously avoids controversy in his editorial efforts is not likely to develop problems with his listeners or with the FCC. It is also unlikely that he will help his community, if he takes the wholly unobtrusive path. The timid licensee, of course, has counterparts in the newspaper field. Norman P. Scott of the Johnstown, Colorado, **Breeze** remarked that, "In the long run, the spineless, fence-straddling editor is but building a Pandora's box, which, when opened, will reveal that he has made enemies of all the thinking readers. They will not be mad at him for what he has said, but will detest him for all he has failed to say."

PROTECTION OF FIRST AMENDMENT

The newspaper publisher who doesn't take strong editorial positions is either a feckless individual who can't stomach controversy, or he is afraid of losing his advertisers and thus his primary source of revenue. The broadcaster, while he may not editorialize for the same reasons, has a more practical argument against voicing his opinions on the air. Not only will he be subjected to possible listener indignation and loss of advertisers, the FCC stands ready to prosecute him for failing to observe the conditions of the Fairness Doctrine or for violating one or more provisions of the Communications Act. The newspaper or magazine publisher may take the position that his publication will remain independent and defend public rights against government, big business, or any other force that threatens the public good. And the publisher can establish such policies with complete impunity under the protection of the First Amendment.

> Congress shall make no law respecting an establishment of religion, or prohibiting the free exercise thereof; or of the press; or of the right of the people peaceably to assemble, and to petition the government for a redress of grievances.

The exclusion of broadcasting from protection of the First Amendment against government interference is one of the most vexatious sociopolitical developments on the American scene. Broadcasters have argued the point from every conceivable position, but Congress has never seriously considered relinquishing its control over the electronic media, clinging to the absurd concept that the airwaves belong to the people and that anyone using those airwaves must be regulated and forced to operate in the "public interest, convenience, and necessity."

47

Many thinking broadcasters prefer to continue the battle to be sheltered by the First Amendment. This is a futile point of view, in the author's opinion. The black man tired of waiting for the white man to amend his laws to make the black man a first class citizen. He marched, picketed, boycotted, created discordance in general, and got action. He took his argument to the people, and that is the only way broadcasters will ever be free to program and editorialize as their conscience dictates. Only by broadcasters pushing for and getting a constitutional amendment will Congress ever turn loose.

The passage of the Federal Election Campaign Act of 1971 (Campaign Communications Reform Act) should be ample evidence for broadcast leaders that the situation won't get better—it will get worse. The Federal Elections Act not only forces broadcasters to accept advertising from persons seeking election to federal office, but also orders broadcasters to sell the time at the end rate in each time classification. Under the old Section 315 of the Communications Act of 1934, licensees at least had the right to refuse to carry political advertising, and were obliged only to charge regular commercial rates when they did accept such advertising. The old rule provided that licensees could refuse political advertising, but that if a station sold time to one candidate in a given race, then all candidates in that race had to be given equal access. In addition, under the Federal Elections Act, broadcasters are forced into additional paperwork. The following form is one legal interpretation of the Act's requirements:

CERTIFICATION

The following Certification under Section 104 (c) of the Federal Election Campaign Act of 1971 must be executed by any candidate for federal elective office (President, Senator, Congressman, Delegate or Commissioner to Congress), or by any person, group, committee, or agency authorized to act on behalf of such candidate, as a prerequisite to the purchase of broadcast time in any primary, general or special election.

Name of candidate:
Political affiliation:

Elective office or nomination sought (include State name where applicable)
Date of election:
Date(s) of use(s) of station:
Duration of each broadcast:
Time of each broadcast:
Rate per broadcast:
Commissions payable:
Total charge:

Joint use? Yes   No

For joint use only:

Percent of total charge attributable to candidate:

Amount of total charge attributable to candidate:

Note: Where a joint use is purchased, the sum of all percentages of the total charge attributable to each candidate must be 100 percent.

I, _____
    Candidate or properly authorized representative

hereby CERTIFY that the foregoing information is true to my knowledge and belief, and further that the expenditure to be made in payment of the above total charge (or that amount of the total charge attributable to the above named candidate if this certificate applies to a joint use) is not in violation of the spending limit of the above named candidate under Section 104(a) of the Federal Election Campaign Act of 1971 and regulations promulgated thereunder by the comptroller general of the United States for the campaign for the above listed nomination or elective office. If I am not the above named candidate, I affirm that I have been authorized in writing by said candidate to make this certification on his behalf.

Date_____ Signed
    Candidate or properly authorized representative **

Section 104(c) of the Federal Election Campaign Act*
of 1971 provides: No station licensee may make any charge

49

for the use of such station by or on behalf of any legally qualified candidate for federal elective office (or for nomination to such office) **unless such candidate (or a person specifically authorized by such candidate in writing to do so) certified to such licensee in writing that the payment of such charge will not violate any (spending) limitation** specified in (the Act)...

(Emphasis added above.)

**When executed by a candidate's representative, a copy of the authorization empowering the representative to certify on the candidate's behalf must be attached to this certificate.

The ORIGINAL and one copy of this certificate are to be retained by the station.

FEAR OF CONTROL

Many licensees simply **fear** the FCC without knowing precisely what it is they fear. It would be unnecessarily embarrassing to identify licensees, particularly those operating in small markets, who have appeared before congressional committees complaining about prohibitions against free programming but who were unable to describe the very restrictions they fear. It should be made clear to the student that written and implied restrictions do exist and that they can be enumerated and must be feared only if the broadcaster is unwilling to endure the agony of compliance.

Control of program content on radio and TV stations essentially is a violation of the American character. Conservative FCC commissioners from the beginning have been criticized by liberals for **failing** to exercise sufficient control over programming. For example, Rep. Paul Rogers (D-Fla.), at the July, 1972, hearings in Washington of the National Commission on Marijuana and Drug Abuse, bitterly assailed FCC Chairman Dean Burch with, "Why haven't you people been more active in studying the effects of socially undesirable advertising? The FCC should be able to tell Congress that there is so much drug advertising on the air, what kind, and "this is our view on the right or wrong effects on people."'

Rogers had long maintained that television advertising of nonprescription drugs, particularly mood-inducing products, subconsciously influences acceptance of the use of drugs to combat life stresses and leads to the use of hard drugs. Chairman Burch pointed out that the FCC is prohibited from controlling program content or editorial judgment.

When the FCC issued the Fairness Doctrine (In the Matter of Editorializing by Broadcast Licensees, June 1, 1949) it said: "We fully recognize that freedom of the radio is included among the freedoms protected against government abridgment by the First Amendment." The Commission then "yeahbutted" its way out of the statement by citing "public rights" and noting that certain requirements for fairness would be mandatory "in the public interest."

While the Commission has defended its failure to strengthen regulations with the First Amendment argument, a number of members have shown a marked indifference to extension of controls. They have been accused of not caring what the American public is subjected to in the way of radio and TV programing. Any commissioner who believes in freedom of the press and places broadcasting in the "press" category must suffer untold agony at the thought of controlling programing. He must relate such administrative and legislative proposals to controlling the printer who is free to print what he pleases. Government officials, both "ins" and "outs," have been critical of the press since the founding of the republic. Former Vice President Spiro Agnew's tirade against the press and broadcast networks is an example of public official hate and distrust of media.

Henry Loomis, a Nixon supporter who was named president of the Corporation for Public Broadcasting in 1972, spoke disparagingly of the TV networks' propensity for commenting on political talks immediately after the talks were finished. "I think 'instant analysis' is lousy because the commentator who is sitting there hasn't had a chance to think." On the other hand, political speeches are so often shaded and contrived that were it not for the "instant analysis" so hated by Loomis, many members of the public indeed would not know what had been said. As for Loomis' comment that commentators hadn't had a chance to think, most network newsmen and commentators make careers of watching and reporting on government and politics. Loomis himself, when asked to head the Corporation for Public Broadcasting, was quoted by **Time** as asking, "What the hell is it?"

It seems unlikely that government will ever voluntarily give broadcasting the same privileges now enjoyed by the press. If the **New York Times** or the **Waxahachie Journal** blasts the President or congress—the only retort is "lies, misinformation, misquote, etc." In the case of a radio station or a television station, the officials can (1) demand and get equal time on the air to reply or (2) work through political channels to put the offending station out of business.

THE FAIRNESS DOCTRINE

The Fairness Doctrine was issued in June, 1949, and represented the FCC's effort to clarify its position with respect to the obligations of broadcast licensees in the fields of news, commentary, and opinion. The document was a result of FCC opinions formed from hearings held in March and April of 1948, hearings that had been initiated by the Commission in September, 1947. Some 49 witnesses from broadcasting, private life, and interested organizations appeared. Further, position statements from 21 others who were unable to attend the hearings were placed in the record. These issues were considered:

1. To determine whether the expression of editorial opinions by broadcast station licensees on matters of public interest and controversy is consistent with their obligations to operate their stations in the public interest.

2. To determine the relationship between any such editorial expression and the affirmative obligation of the licensees to insure that a fair and equal presentation of all sides of controversial issues is made over their facilities.

As a result of studies made on these issues, the Commission issued the Fairness Doctrine. Most of the document was regarded as Commission **policy**, but those parts dealing with personal attacks and political editorials were added to the Commission's **Rules** (73.123, 73.300, 73.598, and 73.679). It is important to the student and licensee to understand his vulnerability to prosecution if the rule is violated. When a station begins editorializing, it should be thoroughly studied in advance.

THE PERSONAL ATTACK RULE

(a) When, during the presentation of views on a controversial issue of public importance, an attack is made upon the honesty, character, integrity, or like personal qualities of an identified person or group, the licensee shall, within a reasonable time and in no event later than one week after the attack, transmit to the person or group attacked (1) notification of the date, time, and identification of the broadcast; (2) a script or tape (or an accurate summary if a script or tape is not available) of the attack; and (3) an offer of a reasonable opportunity to respond over the licensee's facilities.

(b) The provisions of paragraph (a) of this section shall not be applicable (i) to attacks on foreign groups or foreign public figures; (ii) to personal attacks which are made by legally qualified candidates, their authorized spokesmen, or those associated with them in the campaign, on other such candidates, their authorized spokesmen, or persons associated with the candidates in the campaign; and (iii) to bona fide newscasts, bona fide news interviews, and on-the-spot coverage of a bona fide news event (including commentary or analysis contained in the foregoing programs, but the provisions of paragraph (a) shall be applicable to editorials of the licensee).

The Fairness Doctrine is applicable to situations coming within (iii) above and in a specific factual situation may be applicable in the general area of political broadcasts (ii) above.

(c) Where a licensee, in an editorial, (i) endorses or (ii) opposes a legally qualified candidate or candidates, the licensee shall, within 24 hours after the editorial, transmit to, respectively, (i) the other qualified candidate or candidates for the same office or (ii) the candidate opposed in the editorial (1) notification of the date and the time of the editorial; (2) a script or tape of the editorial; and (3) an offer of a reasonable opportunity for a candidate or a spokesman of the candidate to respond over the licensee's facilities; provided, however, that where such editorials are broadcast within 72 hours prior to the day of the election, the licensee shall comply with the provisions of this subsection sufficiently far in advance of the broadcast to enable the candidate or candidates to have a reasonable opportunity to prepare a response and to present it in a timely fashion.

The Fairness Doctrine, obviously, deals not only with editorial matter presented by the licensee, but also with all other broadcasts of a controversial nature. When the licensee permits one or the other side of a controversial issue to be discussed over his facilities, he must, under the doctrine, make an affirmative effort to find spokesmen for opposing points of view. For example, when the licensee accepts paid announcements from a citizens group supporting a bond issue or any other issue of public importance, the licensee must, in his best judgment, present the views of the opposition. He might oppose the issue in an editorial if indeed he does oppose the issue. He might include the opposition's point of view in newscasts, on-the-air news interviews, on a talk show, or he might simply sell or give time to the opposition on a basis calculated to be reasonable and fair. The doctrine does not specify how opposing points of view shall be aired, but the Commission, naturally, is the final administrative arbiter of whether the licensee has been reasonable in his decision. The Commission's Fairness Primer, issued in 1964, is a reliable source of information for the student who wishes to understand how the Commission rules in disputes involving the Fairness Doctrine.

SECTIONS 312 AND 315, COMMUNICATIONS ACT (AS AMENDED)

The passage of the Federal Election Campaign Act of 1971 placed additional regulatory burdens on the licensee, because it significantly amended two sections of the Communications Act. Under the preamended sections, licensees could refuse to carry any political advertising. Under the revision, any licensee is forced, under penalty provided by law, to accept advertising from any politician seeking a federal office.

Furthermore, the amended section requires that "the charges made for the use of any broadcasting station by any person who is a legally qualified candidate for any public office in connection with his campaign for nomination for election, or election, shall not exceed: (1) during the 45 days preceding the date of the primary runoff election and during the 60 days preceding the date of a general or special election in which such person is a candidate, the lowest unit charge of the station for the same class and amount of time for the same period; and (2) at any other time, the charges made for comparable use of the station by other users thereof."

In this amendment, Congress provided that any candidate for any office is entitled to the end rate in any time classification. Not satisfied with this assault on broadcast freedom to decide whether to carry political advertising and charge regular commercial rates should it decide to do so, Congress also addressed itself to the print media:

> "To the extent that any person sells space in any newspaper or magazine to a legally qualified candidate for federal elective office, or nomination thereto, in connection with such candidate's campaign for nomination for, or election to, such office, the charges made for the use of such space in connection with his campaign shall not exceed the charges made for comparable use of such space for other purposes."

Additional amendments to Section 315 require the broadcast licensee to extract a signed statement from the candidate that the payment of charges for broadcast time "will not violate any limitation (on spending) specified in the Campaign Communications Reform Act." Another amendment backs up any state laws dealing with the subject of limitation on campaign expenses, while another provides a fine of $5000 and/or five years in prison for violating the law.

Section 312, as amended, now contains an "access clause" which provides that the Commission may revoke any station license for "willful or repeated failure to allow reasonable access to or to permit purchase of reasonable amounts of time for the use of a broadcasting station by a legally qualified candidate for federal elective office on behalf of his candidacy."

DECISION TO EDITORIALIZE

The licensee, upon deciding to editorialize, should consider some of the following before putting his opinion on the air under the proud banner of **editorial**:

1. Will this editorial help my community?
2. Will it be good for the station?
    a. Will it cost me an advertiser?
    b. Will it cost me a listener?
    c. Who, if anyone, will it offend?
    d. Who, if anyone, will it help?
3. How does the FCC figure into the editorial?
    a. Will anyone ask for equal time?
    b. Should anyone be offered equal time?
    c. Is there a **personal attack** involved?
    d. Am I thoroughly familiar with the Fairness Doctrine?
4. Do I know enough about the subject to voice an opinion?
5. Does anyone on my staff know enough about the subject to voice an opinion?

Some broadcasters, considering such questions, will abandon any idea of putting their opinions on the air. The risk is too great, for some, and the expected gains are too insignificant. One salty editor said that if a station doesn't editorially lose an advertiser once in a while, it isn't doing its job. But the fear of losing business will indeed stop many stations. Lack of researchers has stopped others, while indifference or fear of government reprisal and inability to understand their right to editorialize have been the biggest deterrents. Once the licensee satisfies all the reasons for not editorializing and understands the relatively simple ground rules, he can begin. Fancy language is not required. In fact, Arthur Brisbane urged editorialists to write in a "commonplace and inoffensive way." The essential elements of broadcast editorial are:

1. Introduction: statement of the situation
2. Exposition: plain talk about the facts of the matter
3. Conclusion: the action the editorial suggested.

EXAMPLE

(1) The city council has voted to remove Police Chief John Jackson and replace him with Deputy Chief Orvil Snow. The action was taken against Chief Jackson following his indictment by the grand jury on charges of graft.

(2) Recent news reports quoted mobsters as saying Chief Jackson has received thousands of dollars in payoff money in recent years in return for taking it easy on local gambling operations conducted by the mob. Chief Jackson has denied these charges, but has admitted that there may be some corrupt officers on his police force. Furthermore, Chief Jackson has for years been under attack by some of the liberal elements of this community who favor open saloons, legalized gambling, and other activities which would tend to make our city an open city. Some of these people, along with the mobsters who have been so widely quoted lately, appeared before the grand jury. We don't know what the witnesses told the jury, because the proceedings are secret. One thing we do know is that indictment by a grand jury does not mean Chief Jackson is guilty. And we are beginning to smell a rat.

(3) We think the city's decision to fire Chief Jackson was premature. The grand jury action results only in a charge, not a conviction. Only a court of law can convict, and the grand jury is not a court of law. We have checked Chief Jackson's record and it is a good one. He has held his job for 20 years and, in our opinion, is one of the best law enforcement officers in the state. We think the city council ought to reinstate Chief Jackson immediately. If you, the listener, agree with us, we hope you'll call members of the council and say so.

MEETING REPLY OBLIGATIONS

If the licensee has carefully considered his position **before** airing the editorial, he should experience no difficulty with any social or government forces. In the example above, members of the city council should be sent a copy of the editorial with an offer of reply time. Replies need not necessarily be in the form of a rebuttal editorial. They may take the form of a news interview. For example, the council's position may be voiced by the mayor in a "voicer" handled by the news director.

This radio station today editorially asked the city council to reinstate Police Chief John Jackson. The editorial said the firing of Jackson after he was indicted on graft charges was premature. Mayor Cales Anderson, contacted by our news department, had this to say:

(Voicer prerecorded on tape)

I think the council acted wisely. While it is true that a grand jury indictment doesn't prove a man guilty, we felt that it would be better to remove Chief Jackson from power until after his trial. We felt that the indictment would put a cloud over Jackson's head—and possibly result in his being unable to control all elements of the police force. We don't think the action premature; we're only looking after the best interest of the people.

(End Voicer)

City Councilman Joe Bison said he agreed with Mayor Anderson's assessment of the situation and said further that he thought the entire council would stick together on the issue.

The Fairness Doctrine requires, in essence, that the licensee make a good faith judgment as to whether this sort of news coverage constitutes "fairness." If the licensee aired his opinion six times during a given day, and ran the answering news item once at 3:00 a.m., the Commission, doubtlessly, would rule that the licensee indeed was not fair and that the requirements of the Fairness Doctrine had not been met.

The surest method of meeting Fairness Doctrine requirements is to provide opposing points of view during the same time periods. Rebuttal editorials may be edited to correct fact and length, and to eliminate words and phrases that might constitute libel or slander. But to censor statements that would correctly strengthen the opposition's arguments would result in the licensee having to write additional explanations to the FCC. In the case of a qualified candidate personally answering a station editorial against him, the licensee has **no power to edit.**

Another vehicle commonly used to provide reply time to opposing points of view is the telephone talk show. The moderator might introduce the subject, for example, by saying:

> Tonight we have as our studio guest Mr. G. M. Henshaw, a member of the city council who will defend the council's action in suspending Chief Jackson. Chief Jackson, as most of you know, has been charged with graft by the grand jury and is due to be tried on that charge later this year. Our radio station today said editorially that Jackson should be reinstated. City councilman Henshaw is on our program tonight to explain the council's point of view. After he has said what he came to say, we'll open our telephone lines to listeners for comment and questions. Mr. Henshaw said he'll be glad to field any questions listeners may wish to call in.

LIBEL AND SLANDER

Any licensee undertaking a news and editorial effort should acquaint himself and staff with the laws regarding libel and slander.

Generally speaking, radio and television stations come under the libel laws. But there are variations from state to state; and at the outset of a court fight, state law will prevail. California has a slander law dealing with broadcast matter, while Illinois statutes place broadcasters under libel laws. In Texas, broadcasters generally are not held responsible under Article 5433a (civil statutes) for any defamatory statement published or uttered by someone else in a broadcast "unless it shall be proved by the complaining party, that such owner, licensee, operator, or such agent or employee has failed to exercise due care to prevent the publication or utterance of such statement in such broadcast."

In no event should the editorial writer rely on hearsay or lay counsel (such as that included in this and other texts) in determining whether or not an editorial is libelous. In the final analysis, only a competent attorney, preferably one with specific experience in the field, should be consulted. David McHam of the Journalism Department of Baylor University in Waco, Texas, did a notable study of the subject in his **Law, and the Press in Texas.** The material in this section is drawn primarily from Mr. McHam's work.

Definition

Libel is defamation expressed in oral, written, printed, or any other audible or visible form. It is difficult, if not impractical, to accurately and comprehensively define what constitutes a libel. But the reporter and editorial writer must have an understanding of conditions under which libel (or slander) may occur so that:

1. He may guard against the publication or broadcast of indefensible libelous matter; and
2. In the event of a libel suit being brought, he may provide his employer and himself with a ready means of defense.

The newsman and editorial writer must not mistake freedom of the press and freedom of speech with the law of libel. They are separate doctrines. The first Amendment of the U.S. Constitution says, in part, "Congress shall make no law...abridging the freedom of speech or of the press." Most state constitutions contain similar wording.

Libel laws are not laws of censorship. As a practical matter, anyone can speak, write, draw, or otherwise illustrate or exhibit anything he so desires. He is free to do that. But he must be prepared to face the consequences of libel if the exercise of his freedom infringes on the freedom of another, particularly by damaging his reputation.

Some Background

The law of libel originated as common law. Common law derives its authority from usages and customs of the past and from judgments and decrees of the courts. Before statutory law became prevalent, disputes involving libel were settled in court with previous decisions serving as precedents.

Libel law, therefore, varies from state to state; but in practically every state, the basis of the law is the English common law modified from time to time by statute. In some states, the state legislatures have enacted a substantial body of statutory law.

While the law may be explicit, it cannot cover every possibility. Hence, most libel cases are concerned with issues not directly covered in the statutory law. For example, suppose a suit is brought in Texas by a plaintiff who believes he was injured in some manner by a published (or broadcast) statement. But there is no specific law that says what was published is libel. The case may (or may not) proceed to trial, nevertheless. In such cases, the decision could go either way. When the decision is reached, it provides, in effect, the law that will govern future suits on identical matters to the extent the court involved has influence. In recent years, decisions by the U.S. Supreme Court have greatly altered the common law of libel, particularly as regards the reporting of public acts.

Types of Libel

Basically there are two types of libel. They are:

1. Libel per se, which includes false published statements that—upon their face—bring hatred, contempt, or ridicule upon another. These are determined by case law (previous court rulings) or statutory law.

2. Libel pro quod, which includes false published statements of all kinds resulting in actual injury to another. This type of libel may require an examination of extrinsic facts to make statements defamatory.

For example, calling a doctor a quack, a lawyer a shyster, or a woman a whore are statements that would be libelous per se. Reporting that a woman was declared ineligible for a beauty contest because she was married might be libelous pro quod if one of the conditions for entering the contest was that a woman be unmarried. The reporting of such a fact would indicate fraud or deceit by the woman.

For an action to be initiated, three conditions must be met:

1. The libel must be published.
2. It must be communicated.
3. There must be identification.

The questions of publication and communication are closely related. In fact, a court of civil appeals ruled in an action brought against a Texas newspaper, "It is not necessary to prove that the article was read as that can be presumed."

Radio and television stations may be confronted with a slightly different situation. What is called publication relates also to radio and television broadcasting. But only when something is communicated is there a cause for alarm. The question here may not be whether the libel was broadcast but whether it was seen (on television) or heard (on radio). The point may be a tenuous one, but broadcasters can always hope the people involved weren't listening. A newspaper may be read when it is old, but the broadcast disappears into the airwaves.

Identification is the tricky part. Many newsmen assume that if a name is not used, there is no identification. This is just not true. If any party is able to figure out who the person is, there is identification. Only one person need identify such an unnamed party.

The greater problems dealing with identification are misidentification as in the instance of the similarity of names. The reporter might do well to note that with human nature being what it is, identification is not a complicated matter. Neither is misidentification.

Further Definition

To understand libel, it is necessary to be able to recognize the conditions under which libel may occur. A continual recognition would keep those involved in the coverage and dissemination of news on their toes. Any words are defamatory that:

1. Attack a man's reputation, such as a charge of crime, fraud, dishonesty, immorality, or dishonorable conduct. This may be done directly or indirectly, as by insinuation. It can be done intentionally or accidentally.

2. Expose a person to public ridicule or scorn and deprive him of his right to enjoy normal social contacts. Another way to interfere with a person's rights is to say that he is mentally defective or the victim of a loathsome or contagious disease.

3. Prejudice one in his business or profession.

In other words, the area of concern is quite broad, so broad that any statement that produces an ill opinion of the person may be libelous. Newsmen should constantly remind themselves of this. If a defamatory statement is made, the news medium making the statement must be ready to defend it.

A Misconception

Perhaps the greatest misconception in handling libel is the belief that if someone else says something and the news media report it, the news media are not responsible. If the statement was not privileged, the media bear the blame.

The Libel Equations

Libel is a tort, an offense by one person against another. The redress for libel is in civil courts. There are provisions for criminal libel, all of which are statutory. But in civil libel there is an equation, or formula, by which a person may determine the consequences of a specific libelous remark.

There are three separate steps involved. These may be stated as questions to be asked at the time of publication: Is it libelous? Is it actionable? Is it defensible?

The question of whether a statement is libelous may not be answered until a trial is concluded and maybe not even until appeals have been exhausted. Obviously, though, trials and appeals are costly. Newsmen and their editors may have to decide whether something is libelous before publication. The general rule is, if it is defamatory it is libelous.

Next the question is, is it actionable? This is up to the judge in whose court the case will be heard. He may decide that the statement was not libelous, therefore not actionable, and dismiss the suit. There is no way of knowing in advance what the judge will do. Hence, it is usually best to consider that the statement may be actionable or probably will be actionable.

If the answers to the first two questions have been in the affirmative, then the question is, is the statement defensible? This is the most complicated aspect of libel. But the answer to the question may be derived by logic and reason.

The libel equations go something like this: Not libelous and no defense equal no liability. Libelous and good defense equal no liability. Libelous and no defense equal danger.

Some General Statements

A libelous statement is presumed to be false. At the time of trial, it will not be necessary for the plaintiff to prove that it was false. It has to be defended as true and the burden of defense falls upon the defendant. Such defenses are known as affirmative defenses.

The fact that the statement was published is sufficient to show intent. The difference between willful and negligent intent is of little concern. News media are entrusted with the responsibility of getting things right. Why they didn't is not the issue.

Who is responsible for a libel? The publisher of a newspaper, the licensee of a radio or television station—anyone responsible for writing or editing, printing or selling the product may be held accountable. But the owner is the prime target.

Defenses

Sometimes the definition is given that libel is a defamatory statement published in the absence of a defense. And in the end this is correct.

News media must publish a variety of libelous statements daily. To state that a person has been named in a complaint charging a crime is libelous. To say that a teacher was fired because he was incompetent is libelous. To say that a man has been sued for divorce when the grounds for divorce are infidelity is libelous. But these, and similar statements, are the grist of the news mill. They can be published because even though they are libelous they are defensible. Eight defenses are in common use today. They are:

1. The defense of privilege. Privilege is established primarily by statue. But there is a condition to the privilege. The account must be fair, true, and impartial.
2. The privilege of participants in judicial, legislative, and other official and public proceedings.
3. The defense of truth, or more properly justification. Truth does not mean the literal accuracy of the published account but rather the accuracy of the substance of the account. For example, suppose a reporter wrote that a suspect was wanted for robbery in Baltimore when, in fact, he was wanted for robbery in Dallas. The point is, he is wanted for robbery. This mistake won't hurt.

Young reporters sometimes believe that if they can prove someone said what is in question, it is considered the truth. This does not satisfy the defense of truth. What the speaker says must be proved as true. For instance, suppose a speaker calls someone a thief. It is not necessary to prove that the speaker actually said that. The defendant news medium must be prepared to prove that the party in question is a thief if it publishes the remark.

4. The **New York Times** Rule, the Kansas Rule, or the Public Officer Rule. This is a defense adopted by the statutory law in 15 states, including Kansas, from which it got its name. It was extended to all the states as a result of the ruling by the Supreme Court in **New York Times v. Sullivan.** This defense gives the news media the right to publish false, libelous matter where the plaintiff is a candidate for public office or the holder of a public office, provided the publication is without malice and the falseness arises in good faith and not by design.

5. The defense of consent. A person may not successfully sue for libel based on a communication to which he has consented. The basic example of consent is the publication of what someone says about himself. If a person says something that is incriminatory and he knows it is for publication, he consents to it.

Another example of obtaining consent is informing a person of a charge made against him and presenting him with the opportunity of replying or otherwise making a statement in reply to the charge. Even the denial of the charge may constitute consent.

This is the way unprivileged civil petitions are reported. And the defense of consent may hold even if a person refuses the opportunity to reply and remains silent.

6. Fair comment or criticism. This defense relates only to expressions of opinion as distinguished from statements of fact. It relates to expressions of opinion wherever they may occur, as in editorials, book reviews, sports writing, letters to the editor, and even in advertisements. The matter on which the comment or criticism is made must be of public interest or concern and must be based on facts truly stated. The right to comment and criticism is the right to express opinions on and draw inferences from facts. However, the comment or criticism must be based on facts that are true and can be proved true.

In the matter of reviews, the expertise must be taken into consideration. A cub reporter who knows little about drama does not have the same right to criticize the local civic theater group as an experienced and knowledgeable drama critic. Participants in the arts and sports leave themselves open to criticism of their professional activities. However, their private activities cannot come under the same scrutiny.

The Texas Supreme Court in a 1969 decision ruled that under certain conditions a newspaper is not liable for statements published in its letters-to-the-editor column. The court said there was "no evidence that the defendant published the letter with knowledge that it was false or with reckless disregard or whether it was false or not." However, this was because the court considered the plaintiff to be a public figure, thereby relating the case to the **New York Times** Rule.

7. The right to reply. Courts have held the right to reply as analogous to the right of self-defense. In criminal law, a person who is attacked has the right not only to block the attack but also to use as much force as necessary to repel the attacker. The right to reply enables a person attacked in the public media not only to defend himself but also to attack his attacker with as much force as necessary to repel him. However, he cannot go beyond the bounds of the information at issue, which is to say that his reply must have some relationship to the original attack. Also, the reply must be without malice. This defense provides the news medium with a built-in defense. If it has a controversy raging between two individuals, it becomes merely the vehicle of the attacks. But it must keep open the opportunity to reply or find itself siding with the original attacker and perhaps being the subject of a libel action.

8. Finally, there is the defense involved in the statute of limitations. In all states there is a time limit after which the right to institute action lapses. However, the possibility of recommunication of a libel does exist, which means that the time limit could be extended within the one-year period. This is a far-fetched example, but perhaps possible. Assume that a libelous statement appeared in the newspaper nine months ago. The person libeled in the statement appears in the newspaper office and asks to see a clipping or purchase a copy of the newspaper. With him is a friend and he shows the story to his friend. There is the recommunication of the libel. Newspapers may protect themselves against this by asking persons who want to look at things in their morgues to sign disclaimers.

Additionally, any republication of the libelous matter sets a new time limit. And there is the possibility that republication of a matter defensible at the time of original publication may be without defense. The statute of limitations doesn't provide protection for that.

Partial Defense

Each of the foregoing defenses might be considered complete defenses in the sense that if the arguments behind them prevail, the defendant in the libel action must emerge without judgment against him.

There are also partial defenses, which tend to mitigate or reduce the amount of recovery. If the defendant in the libel action is unable to successfully defend himself with a complete defense, he may introduce any of a number of partial defenses that either show himself in a better light or show the plaintiff in a worse light.

For example, he may introduce testimony that the plaintiff's reputation and character are bad; that because of the general conduct of the plaintiff, it was natural to assume the libelous statement was true and that the circumstances under which the libel was published were such that checking its veracity and authenticity was impossible.

These defenses will not win the case, but they will save some money if argued successfully.

Retractions

One such partial defense is the retraction, which almost everyone agrees shouldn't be called that. Correction is the more acceptable term.

A basic question here concerns when to run a correction and when not to. A good rule to follow is to run a correction only on the advice of a lawyer. Here's the setting: A citizen calls in to say he has been libeled. Whoever answers the phone should be careful not to make any admission of libel. He should be courteous and listen to the complaint. And he should take careful notes on the conversation. The caller should be transferred immediately to someone designated as the proper authority to handle such situations: the news director, the managing editor, the city editor or, in broadcasting, the general manager. News media should not offer to run corrections until the facts are known and there is the determination that libel exists. Frivolous use of corrections can dilute the credibility of the media.

Two situations in which corrections should be offered are when the article in question is factually incorrect and when there is no defense. Other situations might tend to put the medium in a position of admitting to a libel that is not a libel.

Corrections should be handled carefully and, if possible, written under the supervision of a lawyer.

Damages

There are three general classes of damages:

1. Compensatory or general damages, designed to offset the financial injury to the victim of the libel. A libelous statement is presumed to have caused some damage, but the plaintiff will present testimony concerning actual injury, real or imaginary. The most common types of compensatory injury are to business or occupation, to personal reputation, and to the plaintiff, causing him to suffer mentally and physically.

2. Punitive or exemplary damages, also known as vindictive damages, designed as punishment. Actual malice must be proved by the plaintiff. Such damages not only serve as punishment, but also as a warning to the guilty party or parties to be more careful in the basics of journalism.

3. Special damages, which are damages awarded for specific monetary loss incurred by the plaintiff as the result of the publication of statements that are false. They are sometimes known as pecuniary damages. Special damages would be requested in a petition in which the plaintiff claims that false statements have been injurious to him even though such statements are not libelous.

Malice

The term, actual malice, is used to differentiate from legal malice. Legal malice is merely the doctrine that the defendant is responsible for his acts. Actual malice is what costs money in libel suits.

Many defenses for libel are sound only to the point that actual malice is not present. Hence, the danger in malice is that it may eliminate one or all prospective areas of defense. E. Douglas Hamilton, New York libel lawyer and teacher, defines actual malice as "definite behavior on the part of the newsman, either of omission or commission, that deprives the libeled individual of a fair shake." If the case goes to the jury, it is a pretty good bet that one of the questions will be that of malice.

Malice does not mean a feeling of ill will on the part of the newsman toward the individual who claims to have been libeled. The United States Supreme Court gave a definitive explanation of malice in the **New York Times** decision with these words: "Knowledge that it (the published statement) was false or with reckless disregard of whether it was false or not." Also, the court said the plaintiff must be able to prove malice existed with "convincing clarity." Although the **Times** decision dealt with a case involving public officials, it is probable that the court's definition of malice will become the standard.

Special Cases of Libel

Lawbooks are filled with interesting cases of libel that have established precedents related to the common law. A look at some of them is necessary for a full understanding of the effect of court decisions on libel.

Major cases include **Reynolds v. Pegler, Faulk v. Aware, Inc., Butts v. Curtis Publishing Company, Walker v. The Associated Press, Sullivan v. New York Times, Garrison v. State of Louisiana,** and **Rosenbloom v. Metromedia, Inc.** Many of these cases have been reported and analyzed extensively in the daily press, magazines, and books.

Quentin Reynolds' suit against Westbrook Pegler has been covered in at least three books, including **My Life in Court** by Louis Nizer, who was Reynolds' lawyer. **A Case of Libel**, a Broadway play that later was shown on television, was based on the case.

Reynolds' suit was based on a Pegler column on Nov. 29, 1949, that blatantly attacked Reynolds, and on repeated and unremitting attacks by Pegler on Reynolds. The column was prompted by a review Reynolds wrote of a book on Heywood Broun in which he brought up an old feud between Broun and Pegler. The decision in the case—$1 in compensatory damages and $175,000 in punitive damages—indicated Pegler had exceeded the bounds of the right to reply in his attack on Reynolds.

John Henry Faulk's long and involved battle against Aware, Inc. is interestingly recounted in his book, **Fear on Trial.** Faulk was a successful radio and television personality in New York. His Texas humor and folksy satire was often compared to that of Will Rogers. He now makes his home in his native Austin. Incidentally, Nizer was his lawyer, too, and he writes about the case in another of his books, **The Jury Returns.**

Aware, Inc. described itself as "an organization to combat the Communist conspiracy in entertainment-communications." Faulk's suit was based on a February 10, 1956, Aware publication that branded him as a Communist sympathizer. He lost his job with CBS as a result of the publication and was unable to find another in entertainment. By proving ill will, Nizer was able to destroy Aware's defenses of reply and fair comment. On July 16, 1962, the jury awarded Faulk $1 million in compensatory damages and $2.5 million in punitive damages. It was the largest amount involved in a libel verdict to that time. Later, a New York State appellate court, calling the verdict "grossly excessive and most unrealistic," reduced the amount of compensatory damages to $400,000 and punitive damages to $150,000.

Butts v. Curtis Publishing Company and **Walker v. The Associated Press** came out differently, for different reasons, and thereby established standards, particularly in the area of defining public figures and malice.

The Saturday Evening Post published an article on March 23, 1963, alleging that Wally Butts, then athletic director at the University of Georgia, had given information about the Georgia football team to Paul (Bear) Bryant, football coach at the University of Alabama, eight days before the 1962 game between the two schools. The article, which ran under the title "The Story of A College Football Fix," was based on information supplied by a man who said he had been connected accidentally into a long-distance telephone conversation between Butts and Bryant on September 13, 1962. Alabama, a three-point favorite, won the game 35-0.

Neither Butts nor Bryant was contacted by the **Post** or quoted in the article. And at the trial there was testimony that basic information referred to in the article was incorrect. Moreover, several persons denied making statements attributed to them. Testimony also showed that Butts' daughter called the magazine before the article was published, informed the editors that the information was untrue and asked them to withhold the article.

The jury sided with Butts (Bryant also sued; however, Butts' case came to trial first, and Bryant settled out of court) and in 1967 the U.S. Supreme Court sustained the decision. Opinions leaned heavily on the **Post's** failure to report carefully and thoroughly. Chief Justice Earl Warren referred to the magazine's "slipshod and sketchy investigatory techniques." Justice John M. Harlan said the **Post** ignored elementary precautions.

On the same day (June 12, 1967) it returned the Butts decision, the Supreme Court unanimously overturned a $500,000 libel judgment won by Edwin A. Walker, former U.S. Army general, against The Associated Press in a trial in Fort Worth in 1964.

Walker's suit centered around an AP dispatch out of Oxford, Mississippi, giving an eyewitness account of events on the University of Mississippi campus the night of September 30, 1962. A massive riot erupted because of federal efforts to enforce a decree ordering the enrollment of James H. Meredith, a Negro, as a student at the university. The story in question said Walker had taken command of a crowd, estimated at 1000, and had personally led a charge against U.S. marshals who surrounded the Lyceum Building. Walker claimed the statements were false.

The two cases were decided in one opinion. Justice Harlan observed that the activities of Walker were news that required immediate dissemination and that the correspondent "gave every indication of being trustworthy and competent." He said "nothing in this series of events gives the slightest hint of a severe departure from accepted publishing standards."

Of the Butts case, Justice Harlan said that "the evidence is ample to support a finding of highly unreasonable conduct constituting an extreme departure from the standards of investigation and reporting ordinarily adhered to by responsible publishers."

The court established both men as "public figures," a broadening of the "public official" doctrine set out in **Sullivan v. New York Times.** Walker was a public figure because he thrust himself "into the vortex" of a public situation. Butts held a position that commands wide attention and "important responsibility."

But the difference in the cases was in the circumstances of the reporting of the events surrounding the two men, Butts and Walker. Because the **Saturday Evening Post** story constituted a "substantial danger to reputation" without adequate legal proof of the accuracy of the charges, the damages awarded Butts were sustained. Walker lost his case because no malice was shown on the part of the AP or its reporter. The court distinguished between news that required immediate dissemination and a magazine article in which the element of immediacy was lacking. There was no time to check the Walker story, but there was time to check the Butts story.

The trial jury awarded Butts $60,000 in compensatory damages and $3 million in punitive damages in federal court in Atlanta on August 20, 1963. The next January the judge reduced the punitive judgment to $400,000. By the time the money was paid in 1967, interest brought the total to about $572,000. Walker brought 15 actions against the AP and member newspapers, seeking aggregate damages of $33,250,000.

The only other case decided by the time of the Supreme Court ruling was in New Orleans. The $3 million judgment was reduced to $75,000 by a state appeals court. The case was ultimately dismissed. The landmark decision is considered to be the Supreme Court's unanimous reversal of a $500,000 libel judgment against the **New York Times** and four Negro clergymen in Alabama in the case originally styled **Sullivan v. New York Times.** Five public officials in Alabama took offense to a full-page advertisement published in the March 29, 1960, edition of the **Times.** The ad, paid for by friends of Dr. Martin Luther King, Jr., solicited funds for King's defense against charges of state income tax evasion. (He was acquitted.)

The ad stated that police ringed the Alabama State College campus to subdue a student civil rights protest and when the "entire student body" protested, their dining hall was padlocked in an attempt "to starve them into submission." It also charged "Southern violators" with bombing King's home, "almost killing his wife and child," and with arresting him seven times.

L. B. Sullivan, a Montgomery city commissioner who, as commissioner of public affairs, was in charge of the police department, brought suit. And soon afterward so did the mayor of Montgomery, two other city commissioners, and John M. Patterson, then governor. Patterson sought $1 million in damages, the others $500,000 each.

None of the men had been named in the ad, but Sullivan produced witnesses who testified they assumed the wording was intended to mean Sullivan. In separate trials, juries awarded $500,000 judgments to Sullivan and Mayor Earl James. The Sullivan decision was appealed.

The **Times** could not deny that some of the statements were inaccurate. Among them, police had not ringed the campus, the entire student body had not protested, the dining hall was not padlocked, and King had been arrested four times, not seven. Nevertheless, on March 9, 1964, the U.S. Supreme Court overturned the trial court verdict. In the decision the court for the first time found libelous statements protected by the guarantees of the First Amendment. The First Amendment, said the Supreme Court, clearly spells out "a profound national commitment to the principle that debate on public issues should be uninhibited, robust, and wide-open, and that it may well include vehement, caustic, and sometimes unpleasantly sharp attacks on government and public officials."

Two important guidelines, one involving "public officials" and the other defining malice, were established. The court held that the Constitution "prohibits a public official from recovering damages for a defamatory falsehood relating to his official conduct unless he proves that the statement was made with 'actual malice'..." Then the definition for malice was given: "that is, with knowledge that it was false or with reckless disregard of whether it was false or not."

Although the plaintiff was recognized as a "public official," the court did not identify the extent of the term: "We have no occasion here to determine how far down into the lower ranks of government employees the 'public official' designation would extend...or otherwise to specify the categories of persons who would or would not be included."

Regarding the term "actual malice," the court said the mere presence of material in the files of the **New York Times** showing the falsity of certain statements in the advertisement did not constitute the framework for malice. Failure to check the files, the court said, was at most, negligence. Recklessness must mean something more than the mere failure to follow basic reportorial and editing procedures.

Four months after the **Times** decision, the defamation of a public official was again before the Supreme Court, this time in a criminal libel case: **Garrison v. State of Louisiana.** Jim Garrison, district attorney of Orleans Parish, was feuding with eight New Orleans criminal judges. At a news conference he accused the judges of, among other things, refusing to give their approval for pay to undercover agents and said the refusal raised "interesting questions about the racketeer influences on our eight vacation-minded judges."

The judges charged him with criminal defamation, a misdemeanor that, in Louisiana, required no jury trial. Garrison was convicted, sentenced to a $1000 fine and four months in jail. He appealed. The Supreme Court reversed the conviction and extended to criminal libel the theory behind the **Times** opinion. Justice Hugo Black said, "There is absolutely no place in this country for the old, discredited English Star Chamber law of seditious libel."

Over the years, Justice Black seized every opportunity to speak out in libertine fashion against the whole concept of libel. In connection with decisions returned by the court in February, 1971, he wrote: "As I have stated before, it is time for this Court to abandon **Sullivan v. New York Times Company** and adopt the rule to the effect that the First Amendment was intended to leave the press free from the harassment of libel judgments."

On June 7, 1971, the U.S. Supreme Court held that the standard applied to a public official or a public figure applies also to a private individual when he becomes involved in an event of public interest. In a 5-3 vote the court held that the free flow of information would be jeopardized by even the fear of libel suits for falsehoods about persons who involuntarily are caught up in news reports of events "of the public or general interest."

The case, **Rosenbloom v. Metromedia, Inc.**, grew out of news broadcasts over radio station WIP in Philadelphia, Pennsylvania. The station carried stories of the arrest of George A. Rosenbloom for possession of obscene literature. Later stories concerned Rosenbloom's lawsuit against certain officials alleging that the magazines he distributed were not obscene and seeking injunctive relief from police interference with his business. These latter stories did not mention Rosenbloom by name but used the terms "smut literature racket" and "girlie-book peddlers." Upon his acquittal in state court of criminal obscenity charges, Rosenbloom sued the radio station for libel. The jury found for him, but the decision was reversed by the court of appeals and upheld by the Supreme Court.

CHAPTER 6

Ways and Means of Editorializing

At many radio stations, operations such as the "traffic department," the "production department," or the "engineering department" are handled by one person. One can find little of this objectional if a single worker realistically performs the work. Similarly, an editorial department may involve only the licensee or general manager (wearing another hat, of course), or it may involve a half dozen specialists whose combined effort produces a more substantial result.

Size in itself does not imply quality. William Allan White proved this truism with his hell-raising editorials in The Emporia (Kansas) **Gazette**. White was known as the "Sage of Emporia" and in 1923 he won the Pulitzer Prize for editorial writing. One of his editorials, "What's The Matter with Kansas?" was reprinted and distributed by the Republican Party and is given considerable credit in the election of William McKinley as President of the United States.

A daytime radio operation in a market of 5000 can do a decent editorial if the licensee is sincerely interested in his community. At minimum, he can read wire stories and out-of-town newspapers, then take safe-distance pot shots at state and national governments. It is doubtful that such expressions will be productive, but they might generate a few more letters to representatives in government.

Should the licensee remain "independent" of party factions? Or should he join his version of the "good guys" and push a particular philosophy? The independent licensee, of course, remains free to criticize both the "ins" and the "outs" in government affairs. But the licensee who is aligned with one side or the other often has greater editorial clout because of his more intimate knowledge of transpiring events. This decision is strictly up to the individual broadcaster and his conscience.

Gordon McLendon never editorially embraced a political party, although his editorials consistently support a conservative point of view. He ran for the U.S. Senate as a conservative against the left-wing candidate, Sen. Ralph Yarborough. While his conservative philosophy was expressed in most of his editorials, McLendon simply was never able to fully accept either national party or align himself with local or state political factions. The conservative thinking or the race for the U.S. Senate did not take McLendon off the list of "independents." He still felt free to criticize anyone whose views he opposed.

The small-town newspaper editor or publisher is faced with essentially the same problems of how to write and publish effective editorials with a small staff and whether to remain independent. His big-city counterpart has a staff of editorial writers with private offices and virtually unlimited sources of information. In many cases, these editorialists are aged reporters who have been stashed away in an editorial office to finish out their active days before retirement. The prose of these ancients is sometimes incomprehensible, but it does fulfill the paper's commitment to publish the traditional editorial page. A major market managing editor once said, "Yeah, ol' Joe's still around; he writes that column every day. But I'll be darned if I can understand what he's talking about." This is not to condemn such departments to total mediocrity; most major dailies have a staff of young, hard-working journalists who turn out timely, incisive editorials that expose, cajole, argue, and in general, perform the mission that editorial pages are supposed to perform.

The small-town licensee or publisher has a **responsibility** to perform to the extent possible the roles played by big-city operations. It simply is not enough to resign the proffered leadership by claiming, "I just don't have the time."

While many editorial writers have reportorial backgrounds, such training and experience **are not** essential in the writing and distribution of broadcast **or** newspaper editorials. The licensee with a news background may feel more at home in such work, but the only really essential characteristic required of an editorial writer is the good sense to recognize a community problem and the stomach to get on the air and talk about it. Some stations whose management has neither time nor talent for editorializing simply hire an outside writer to research and write editorials. In many markets there are news reporters anxious to pick up extra money for this kind of work.

The licensee who understands his obligations under FCC rules and policies may take to the air as fearlessly as his newspaper counterpart, regardless of education and training. If he simply has the desire to become a community leader via the editorial route, he need only read the rules and prepare for some paperwork before opening his microphone. The goals and philosophies of the one-man "editorial department" are no different from those of the multimillion dollar facility that can afford the manpower and talent of a large department. The optimum editorial department described here does not exist; it has been pieced together from many stations with the idea of creating a model entity that would be viable for medium to large stations, yet serve as a guide for the small-market licensee who couldn't possibly afford the personnel or equipment.

A PUBLIC AFFAIRS DEPARTMENT

Our hypothetical city has a population of slightly over one million. There are three VHF TV stations affiliated with the major networks, along with one independent VHF and two UHF stations. Channel 13 is a Public Broadcast Corporation facility. Sixteen AM and FM radio stations serve the market with primary signals, while stations in 20 other service areas send "listenable" signals into the city. None of these facilities has ever broadcast a serious editorial, and the city's second largest daily newspaper has merged with its only competitor.

The commonly owned morning and afternoon dailies, under terms of the merger agreement, continue to produce two newspapers, but in the same plant and under the editorial direction of a single publishing entity. The city administration has been elected year after year by the Citizens for Good Government Association (CGGA). No progressive candidate has ever stood a chance at the polls, so deeply entrenched are the leaders of CGGA. The directors of the corporation that publishes the city's commonly owned newspapers are old stalwarts of CGGA and have had their hands on the city's government throttle for 25 years. The city council, under the benevolent and paternal guidance of CGGA, has managed to fight off proposals to modernize everything from the police department to the city pound. The CGGA leaders have quietly but effectively let it be known to intruders that "this is our town and we plan to run it like we've always run it."

One of the major VHF TV licensees also owns an AM-FM operation and has completed his study of community problems, as required by the FCC. The licensee's call letters are KXXX-TV-AM-FM and he is considered an "outsider" by the CGGA. The community survey, conducted primarily by the licensee and his three general managers, involved 200 so-called "community leaders" from all walks of community life. It reveals the following problems and complaints:

1. Inadequate and insufficient city recreational facilities.
2. Air pollution caused primarily by two local industries.
3. Unlawful "executive sessions" held by city council.
4. Local newspapers always back the city administration, often failing to even mention its political opponents.
5. Inequities in property evaluation policies.
6. City shows discrimination in employment practices.
7. Police scandals have been hushed up by city and print media.
8. City administration rules school board with iron hand.
9. City administration has refused to match federal funds for construction and equipment.
10. City employs questionable methods in awarding construction contracts.

Dozens of other problems involving low-cost housing, mass transportation, low-quality and high-cost public utilities, and poverty are mentioned both by community "leaders" and members of the general public who were surveyed. But the 10 problems enumerated above were cited most often by those interviewed. The licensee, recognizing his responsibility to offer programing that will at least "aid in the solution" of the problems, decides there are too many unsolved problems in his community and that perhaps he'd better devote more of his stations' time to them. Furthermore, he has heard that a group of fellow "outsiders" may challenge him when he files for license renewal on grounds that he (and the other local broadcast facilities) have not served the needs and interests of the citizens in his service area. In view of the situation, he lays down the following plan of action to his general managers:

GOALS

KXXX's purpose in establishing a public affairs department is to provide the citizens in our coverage area with another editorial point of view and a medium through which some of the community's most pressing problems can be openly and honestly discussed. The department will be charged with the responsibility of (1) investigative reporting, (2) developing news and editorial material for airing, (3) seeking out competent opposition, (4) preparing and scheduling public service announcements, (5) conducting a continuing survey of community problems, and (6) developing the means by which KXXX can solve the problems via on-the-air facilities or otherwise. When necessary, KXXX will purchase space in local print media to conduct surveys among nonlisteners and will prepare and distribute brochures that reflect not only the extent to which we pursue public affairs work but also put into writing for the benefit of the community the findings of the department. In general, the department will become the citizen's ombudsman and gadfly (gadfly is defined as a person who stirs up from lethargy or annoys). We want to annoy the people in this city who try to make government a "private thing." There are no areas of government or society that are sacrosanct and we will explore all of them.

An informal editorial board will be membered by the three general managers, the news directors, program directors, and the licensee. The board will approve all editorials before they are aired, and will suggest editorial and public affairs topics for consideration by the editorial director. The board will have few if any formal meetings. Proposed editorials and public affairs projects will be circulated until each member has voiced his opinion. The licensee will have the final word on all editorial subjects.

ORGANIZATION

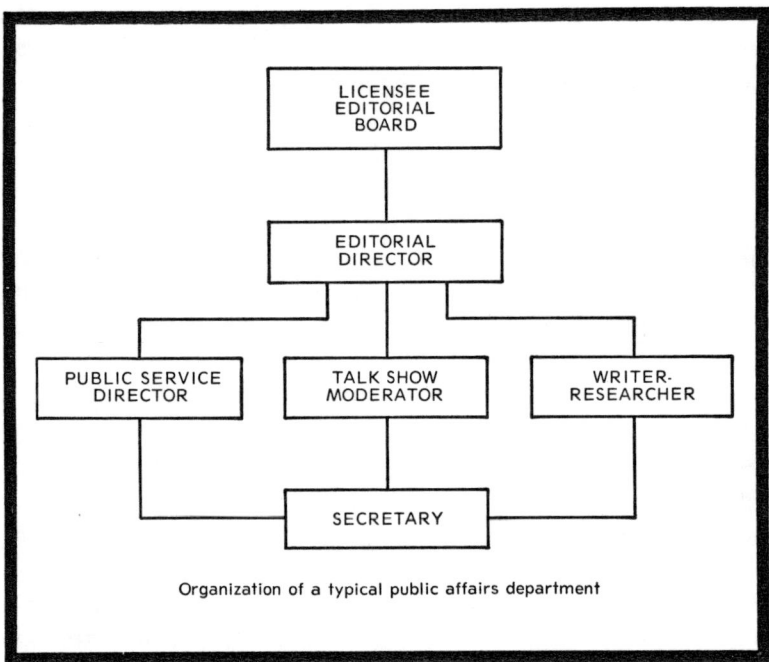

Organization of a typical public affairs department

The public affairs department will be managed by the editorial director, who will be equal in rank with other department heads (news director, program director, etc.) and who will report directly to the general manager of KXXX-TV. The staff will include the public service director, a talk show moderator, a writer-researcher, and a secretary. Resources of the news and program departments will be available to the editorial director.

Editorial Director

This person should have a background in journalism, public relations, political reporting, and a thorough knowledge of the community and its social and political life. Age, sex, race, or religion will not be a consideration in management's selection. The person must be well founded in FCC rules and policies concerning editorializing and public affairs programing. The editorial director's job, essentially, is to execute the policies set forth in this "ways and means" memorandum. He will supervise the work of the public service director, talk show moderator, writer-researcher, and secretary. In addition, he will personally develop material for editorials, editorial campaigns, and documentaries.

Talk Show Moderator

Background should include experience in handling a talk show. This person must be well read and have a deep understanding of basic human problems. He or she must be highly articulate and be able to inoffensively weed out the "time wasters" who call. The talk show moderator will work directly with the editorial director and the editorial board in developing subjects for discussion on the nightly talk show. The moderator has a responsibility to management to ascertain that both sides of any controversial issue are aired. The moderator will take the opposing view from time to time. When this is not practical, the moderator will bring guests into the studio to speak for the opposition. This failing, the moderator will arrange to have the opposition call the show and express their views. The moderator will undertake no "campaigns" without approval of the editorial director and the editorial board. While management recognizes that a moderator of a talk show must express his own opinion from time to time, the moderator must understand that he primarily is a referee of a public discussion between station listeners.

Public Service Director

Background should include journalism, civic and social work, some experience as a secretary, and a public speaker. The public service director will make affirmative efforts to develop on-the-air public service campaigns. This will include

83

setting up a list of organizations and institutions that are needful of air time and working with local leaders to develop meaningful and productive announcements. No "canned" PSAs will be aired. Every PSA aired will be local or have a local angle, and will be produced in KXXX's production room under direction of the PSD. The public service director will accept public speaking invitations and express station management's points of view, as well as attend other meetings at which important public issues will be discussed.

Writer-Researcher

Background must include experience in newspaper or broadcast reporting, formal training in journalism, and an ability to dig for the facts of a given situation and report them accurately. Experience in police reporting or investigation will be helpful. The person will work at the direction and under supervision of the editorial director. The responsibility includes researching and writing editorials as well as data papers for use by the talk show moderator. A writer-researcher should be capable of taking charge of campaigns involving on-camera interviews on location and in the studios.

Secretary

Background must include experience as secretary, preferably in broadcasting or government. A secretary must possess all secretarial skills and be available to work overtime and on weekends and holidays. Duties include correspondence for all members of the department, the maintenance of department files, assistance in research and writing, when necessary, and ascertainment that every member of the editorial board has approved editorials before they are produced for airing. The secretary will coordinate with radio and television program personnel in scheduling and broadcasting editorials and public affairs programs.

Such detailed outlines, obviously, are not essential to a successful and productive editorial effort. Many of the licensees and managers interviewed for this text had no such formal or pronounced policies. They simply assume roles of leadership in their communities and go forward with their duties. The ways and means of editorializing, essentially, lie within the licensee.

CHAPTER 7

The Editorial

The writing and production of a broadcast editorial does not require genius, but it does demand spirited motivation and logical purpose. Why should the editorial be aired? E. L. Godkin of The Nation advised, "Never write anything without conveying information or expressing an opinion with reasons." Gordon McLendon said, "Editorials should stir people to action." Peter Straus said the licensee should write editorials that "take strong positions and suggest actions." Arthur Brisbane, one of the first syndicated newspaper columnists in the United States and an editor for Hearst newspapers, said, in 1912, that an editorial should "teach, defend, attack, praise. It should interpret, influence opinion, entertain." Brisbane said editorials should inform, not incite; interpret, not indoctrinate. "They should prod, question, criticize, clarify, refine, reject, recommend, demand, and expose. They should precede public opinion and accelerate its pace, point out the inconsistencies of public men, and start a train of thought."

It is not always easy to discern such characteristics in broadcast or newspaper editorials. Indeed, many of them sound like exercises in semantics, undisguised efforts to meet a public affairs programing commitment, or simply splice meaningless type into the editorial columns. Not rarely, there is more editorial matter in the newscasts and news columns than in those vehicles specifically designed for the expression of opinion.

KINDS OF EDITORIALS

David Dary, in his Radio News Handbook, describes six different types of editorials:

Informative   Call-for-action

Interpretative   Persuasive

Argumentative   Entertaining

To these, we might add accusative and emotional, and note that in many cases two or more of the classifications are required to describe a given editorial. A personal attack editorial might include all but the entertainment classification. The hypothetical Chief Jackson editorial (chapter 5) falls primarily into the "argumentative" category, inasmuch as it argues that the city council action was premature. While the editorial did call for action by asking listeners to call city councilmen, its major thrust was argumentative. A prime example of a persuasive-call-for-action editorial was written by Gordon McLendon in November, 1963, and aired over KLIF in Dallas. It also was printed in the Dallas *Times Herald* on November 26, 1963. Dallas had been scalded by the national press following President Kennedy's assassination. McLendon, in a strained but still strong voice, delivered the editorial.

DEEP SORROW BUT NO SHAME

The day of mourning has passed. It is time to take up the business of the day again.

As we found in visiting Cleveland and Chicago Sunday, Dallas will need to defend itself in many quarters. Let us begin, then, with a vigorous defense of the Dallas Police Department. To eastern criticism, we say that Dallas has one of the nation's finest police forces. Dallas is one of the nation's cleanest cities. There are no payoffs, no rackets, no bribes—an extremely low incidence of violence. In Dallas, there is little of the corruption that has run like cancer through the police departments of Chicago and Boston and Philadelphia. The unexplainable appearance of Lee Harvey Oswald's killer at police headquarters has happened many times elsewhere. How did the police at Buffalo let Czolgoss get so close to President McKinley? How did the police of Washington let Guiteau get so close to Garfield? How did the Miami police allow Guiseppe

Zangera to kill Mayor Cermak of Chicago and almost kill Franklin Roosevelt? How could Washington police allow that tragic moment at Ford's Theater? How did the police of Milwaukee allow a would-be assassin to shoot President Theodore Roosevelt?

So, to the eastern critics of Dallas police, we say that where there is life, there is always human error. We further say to other cities, many of them hotbeds of police corruption, clean your own house first. Ours is already clean. Let the defense of Dallas begin right here. All Texans should rise indignantly and affirmatively to the defense of this state and city.

Stand up and be counted. We need have deep sorrow, but no shame.

In this case, it is doubtful that McLendon entertained any thought of offering reply time to anyone. The central theme of the editorial was to **persuade** the country to take a closer look at Dallas and not blame the city and its citizens for the death of the young president. The call-for-action element was relegated to an insignificant role in the editorial.

An example of an informative-argumentative editorial that calls for action was broadcast in April, 1972, by WAVZ in New Haven, Connecticut. In this example, the introduction and close are included:

> We take you now to the editorial room of WAVZ for a statement of opinion by this station. Here is Daniel W. Kops, president of Kops-Monahan Communications, Inc., to bring you that statement.
>
> Thank you.
>
> Mayor Guida has been playing a strong leadership role in shaping up the redevelopment commission, including designation of a new director. The goals he has announced for that phase of the city's operations are all for the good.
>
> And, in this light, we find it impossible to understand his turning his back on the school board, while that board proceeds with petty politicking which is driving away a highly respected superintendent of schools.

If the mayor can bring his influence to bear on one agency, he can do as much with the board of education, including calling for the resignation of members of the board who are making life untenable for Superintendent Jerry Barbaresi.

For the second time in hardly a year, citizens and groups representative of many walks of life have spoken out in favor of Jerry Barbaresi. He has built bridges between people of different backgrounds. He has been a good administrator. The only suggestion we have had as to how he has displeased some members of the board is his unwillingness to make political patronage more important than competence in appointments within the system.

It's just possible the mayor could still save the day, and we hope he will.

Thank you for your attention.

You have been listening to a WAVZ editorial, a statement of opinion by this station.

Television has an infinitely greater capacity to dramatize editorial messages than radio and newspapers. Station WCBS-TV, in what may be described as an "informative-interpretative" editorial, used a production technique that in itself helped make the editorial viewpoint. The editorial employed videotape excerpts from speeches delivered by President Nixon and former Vice President Agnew. Peter Kohler, director of editorials for WCBS-TV, did the "voice over video tape" portions of the editorial, while the Nixon and Agnew portions were taken from news film or videotape.

FEVER OF WORDS

VOICE OVER VIDEO TAPE: The day was January 20, 1969, the inaugural of Richard Nixon as President of the United States. It was a day for inspirational words, for eloquent words, but words hard to recall through the divisive din of the political campaign just past.

PRESIDENT NIXON: (Clip from Inaugural Address)

Greatness comes in simple trappings. The simple things are the ones most needed today if we are to surmount what divides us, and cement what unites us...

VICE PRESIDENT AGNEW: (Clip from speech made In San Diego, Calif., Sept. 11, 1970)

In the United States today we have more than our share of the nattering nabobs of negativism.

PRESIDENT NIXON: (Clip from Inaugural Address)

To lower our voices would be a simple thing. In these difficult years, America has suffered from a fever of words; from inflated rhetoric that promises more than it can deliver; from angry rhetoric that fans discontents into hatreds; from bombastic rhetoric that postures instead of persuading...

VICE PRESIDENT AGNEW: (Clip from speech made in Phoenix, Arizona, October 9, 1970)

Listen to this, this is an odd quote, "You have a God-given right to kick the government around." Senator Muskie said that during the 1968 campaign, and, he added, don't hesitate to do so. The senator, I am sure, was not advocating physical violence, but such language gives respectability to the urging of others. It's a short step from kicking the government around to kicking the police around.

PRESIDENT NIXON: (Clip from Inaugural Address)

We cannot learn from one another until we stop shouting at one another, until we speak quietly enough so that our words can be heard as well as our voices...

VICE PRESIDENT AGNEW: (Clip from speech in Salt Lake City, Utah, October 1, 1970)	Please don't contribute to the Spock-marked generation. Please don't contribute to the kind of climate in this country that raises emotion beyond reason. Listen, argue, denote, condemn where you must. But do it with your mind, not with your butt.
VOICE OVER VIDEO TAPE:	America has suffered from a fever of words and passions, from the obscenities shouted by demonstrators at the President during several campaign stops, including this one in San Jose, California, in the closing days of the campaign. Later, when the Presidential motorcade departed San Jose, it was stoned, a reprehensible act.
	(END VIDEO TAPE)
VOICE:	But America's fever of words was also brought on by the angry and bombastic rhetoric of Vice President Agnew and by the President himself, when they sought to link their political opponents with ugly mobs, with violence. And it was this kind of campaign tactic, we believe, that not only exploited the very violence it condemned, but which also mocked the spirit of the inaugural, those eloquent phrases about lowering voices and surmounting what divides us and cementing what unites us.

This editorial not only falls into the "informative" and "interpretative" classifications, but also touches on the accusative and, for some, entertaining. The production techniques were designed to get and hold viewer attention as well as help explain the editorial point of view.

The "emotional" type editorial is probably more prevalent than surveys indicate. These are the kind licensees and publishers alike run on spur-of-the-moment impulse, such as this one from KTVU, San Francisco-Oakland.

MUNICH

> The most reprehensible crime of mankind is political murder, whether it takes place in Vietnam, in South America, or in the United States. But the willingness to use murder to hijack the Olympics in Munich for political ends is a special case. Arab nationalism as a motive is a copout. The guerrillas were political gangsters, and their act of arrogance was without a shred of nobility.
>
> To use up the lives of the innocent and politically uninvolved to advance one's own political cause is such a crime against humanity, it should have the death penalty as an option.

While McLendon's "deep sorrow" editorial reeked of emotionalism, it also resulted from considerable research which informed listeners and asked for a response. The KTVU editorial simply said what most citizens were thinking and saying about the Munich affair. McLendon, at other times, ran editorials eulogizing friends or high-ranking public officials who had died. There is nothing wrong, per se, with these emotion-charged editorials, but they should be held to a minimum lest the public be fooled too often into thinking an upcoming editorial is important to the public welfare. In the cases cited, the "deep sorrow" editorial was so eloquently phrased and articulated that it said so much better what many were thinking. The "Munich" editorial, in its utter rage, would echo the sentiments of most who saw and heard it.

Humorous editorials are rare among stations that editorialize, but some licensees can't resist the whimsical urge to broadcast a "light-hearted" editorial on everything from computers to women's lib to men's fashions. This effort on the part of Homer Lane of KOOL-TV-AM-FM, Phoenix, Arizona, is an example.

MACHINES

We sometimes feel that our quest for efficiency has resulted in our working for the machines we created, rather than the machines lightening our labor.

Remember last Tuesday's election when we all had to wait for hours for the computer to tell us who we nominated? Or have you ever tried to correspond with the computer that figures how much you owe the department store or the gasoline company? Then there is our new car. It imperiously commands us to fasten our safety belt or listen to it buzz until we do. If we leave the car for a moment and do not remove the ignition key, the car calls us back and commands us to remove the key, even if we are only stepping to the mailbox on the corner. Oh yes, if we want to leave on our headlights to find the keyhole at the front door, the car is insulted and sets up a wail until we return to douse the lights.

There are times when we long for the days when a human being checked our tax returns and not a machine; when we drove a car and it was ours to command, instead of feeling like a guest who has lapsed into bad manners and has offended our own machine. The day we must risk being stifled by a mandatory air bag may be the day when we trade our mechanical master for a ten-speed bike, although we doubt if the cars will permit us on the streets our tax dollars bought.

This editorial accomplished absolutely nothing, except perhaps to draw a few chortles and nodding agreements. It has the flavor of a Will Rogers commentary, as opposed to a licensee-endorsed editorial that explains, questions, accuses, cajoles, demands, or advocates. One advantage to a humorous editorial is that reply time is rarely indicated, although one wag did tell Homer Lane of KOOL that a local computer was planning to ask for reply time under terms of the Fairness Doctrine.

Station KNXT in Los Angeles broadcast an "accusative" editorial in September, 1972, which technically constituted a "personal attack" against two U.S. athletes in the 1972 Olympics in Munich. The editorial was written by editorial director Howard Williams.

MATTHEWS AND COLLETT

Vince Matthews and Wayne Collett have been thrown out of the Olympics.

When Collett and Matthews took their medals for placing one-two in the 400-meter sprint, they made an obvious display of disdain for their National Anthem. They also insulted the concept of Olympic sportsmanship.

Apparently they realized very quickly that they were in trouble and they began to deny any intentional insult. But who can believe that in view of their other statements of disrespect for the United States?

If they have so little regard for the United States, why did they want to go anyway? They're entitled to their opinions, but it was two-faced of them to accept places on the team representing the United States. They used their position, and their medals, to take a cheap shot at their country.

They can think what they like, but the Olympics is no place to mix in their politics. There's been too much of that in Munich already.

The Olympic Games are a place for international friendship and sportsmanship of the highest order. The boos and jeers of the crowd in the stadium showed them that the rest of the world didn't like what happened either.

We like to see American athletes win—but win, lose, or draw, we want them to uphold the spirit of the Olympic Games.

This editorial is a classic in style, directness, clarity, and poignancy. It combines the writer's anger, wrath, research, and intelligence into an editorial that says something critical but constructive about a condition that touches the sensitivities of many citizens. Station KNXT has used the same bold, incisive approach on local issues.

These examples should indicate that any licensee with normal intelligence who is motivated by a sense of community can editorialize effectively, without researchers and writers and without having to bear the cost of a news or editorial department. The following hypothetical example illustrates how the overworked and financially hard-pressed licensee might handle an editorial on a local issue.

WET-DRY ELECTION

As we make our run up and down the streets of Smalltown, we keep hearing stories of how certain people are planning to vote for the legal sale of alcoholic beverages. We don't know who these "wets" are, and don't care.

Smalltown is a good place to live and a good place to raise children. Our schools may not be the best in the state, but they're not the worst either. This radio station opposes the sale of beer, wine, and whiskey in Smalltown. We're not a drinking community; we're a church-going community, by and large, and we here at the radio station can't see how legalizing the sale of alcohol will help anything. Those who drink have for years driven to the neighboring county for their booze—and the system seems to have worked okay.

We'd like to see the churches and the school organizations get together and really fight to keep alcohol out of Smalltown. If we go to sleep at the wheel, we're liable to wake up some morning and find open saloons operating next to our schools and churches.

This radio station is obligated to provide free time to the opposition when one side of a public issue is discussed on the air. If anyone wants to come out in favor of legalizing the sale of booze in Smalltown, they're welcome. At least we'll know who the decent citizens of the town are up against.

The example is, perhaps, an oversimplification. The editorial indicates no research, no skilled rhetoric, and none was required. The licensee simply felt strongly about the subject and used his facilities to express his opinion. Airing of the editorial represented the leadership role the broadcaster can and should take, whenever the opportunity arises. The editorial might have been better had the licensee been able to cite statistics indicating a heavy crime rate in the neighboring county where alcoholic beverages were sold, but this would have taken time which he didn't have. He might have dug further and determined that the neighboring county had more automobile accidents than Smalltown's county; but, again, time was the determining factor.

If a small-market licensee has enough gumption to apply for and receive a license, he certainly has enough intelligence

95

to comment on events of the day in his service area. While there are few major markets with competing daily newspapers, there are virtually no small markets with even competing weeklies. In many such instances, there is one small, aging weekly paper and a low-power daytime-only radio station. The licensees of such stations, regardless of education, ability, and finances, have an obligation to take editorial points of view, if only to express differences with the local newspaper. Of course, there is no legal obligation for the licensee to editorialize. But the author's view is that the licensee is derelict in his moral duty if he doesn't exert every possible effort at using his vacility in a community leader role.

HOW TO WRITE AN EDITORIAL

The key to writing an effective editorial that communicates an idea is simplicity. The famous William Buckley of New York is regarded as a brilliant thinker and writer. But his work is so crowded with unfamiliar words, independent clauses, abstract thinking, and classic references that normally or poorly educated citizens often may as well try to understand a column written in a foreign language. McLendon has been guilty of writing and speaking above the heads of his audience. He once bawled out an editorial assistant for "using words strange to listeners." "You've got to keep your editorials simple if you expect to be understood," he explained. The very next day, McLendon used the word "detente" in an editorial and was immediately called to task by chortling assistants. "Well," McLendon reasoned, "you have to give them a new word now and then."

Quintilian, the Roman instructor of rhetoric, said that "to the erudite, we cut to the bare facts. To the illiterate, we must paint clearer pictures." Thus, he implied the need for explicit detail and "picture words" that make the point.

There is a wide range of difference between writing for the eye and writing for the ear. Radio editors for the wire services probably were the first to learn and then teach the variations. The stilted, old five-Ws (who, what, where, why, and when) lead of journalism wouldn't work in broadcasting. Sentences that ended in "he said"—after rambling on endlessly for 30 or 40 words—simply left announcers gasping for breath and wondering what they'd just said. The same principle applies in editorial writing, of course, except that there must be (and can be) greater simplicity in broadcast editorials than in a broadcast news story. Here is one example of how an "involved" editorial may be simplified.

BAIL BONDS

Wrong	Correct
Judge Lewis Schmidt of the 146th District Court—which last week was the scene of a legal battle in which a bail bondsman slugged an attorney from the district attorney's office—has stated privately that he believes most local bondsmen are operating illegally.	A local district judge believes most of Ourtown bail bondsmen are operating illegally.
Judge Schmidt, who is not up for reelection this year, has, in effect, indicted every bail bondsman in the area with his off-the-bench charge. We know of instances where bondsmen are scrupulously honest and have adequate cash and real estate to back up every bond they endorse.	KXXX knows this is not true; Judge Lewis Schmidt's statement was an unfair indictment of many bondsmen who scrupulously observe the letter and the spirit of the law.
There is no doubt in our minds that some bondsmen have solicited business within the jails and that they have deliberately falsified statements as to their liquid assets. We do not condone such action and we editorially urge the district attorney to take action. But neither can we believe that a district judge with a high public trust could slam a condemning fist down on	We know some bondsmen break the rules. And the guilty ones should be dealt with by the district attorney. Judge Schmidt should retract his statement to restore public faith in those honest bondsmen who provide a bona fide service to citizens in trouble.

97

a sizable number of good citizens in order to get at one or two guilty ones. The charge was unpardonable and Judge Schmidt should retract his statement.

Most editorials studied run one to three minutes in length. There were exceptions, of course, but most editorialists believe they cannot hold listener attention for more than two minutes with such material. Further, "comment" on most public issues can be accomplished in a short period of time as the best editorials deal with only one subject. The same principle applies to a good commercial, which rarely runs more than 60 seconds. The editorial that deals with an intricate situation involving several persons and two or more organizations often cannot be delivered within a prescribed period of time. And the editorial writer shouldn't be forced to conform to a time limitation when he's attempting to "communicate" an idea to an elusive listening or viewing audience. Most opinions can be stated in less than a minute on any given subject, but occasionally more time is needed to provide background and explain the "whys" of a particular point of view.

While the broadcaster who engages in editorializing has learned to keep them short and to the point, respondents with differing points of view have not. They often require help in rewording and rephrasing rebuttals. The station should provide such assistance with the objective of giving listeners a clear picture of both or several sides of the issue under discussion.

DELIVERY

Realistically, the editorial should be delivered by the person writing it. The "reader" should not only understand the words of the editorial, but also be able to provide the necessary voice inflections to emphasize or deemphasize certain points. Copy interpretation is critically important if the listener or viewer is to get the message. The announcer who simply reads the words will be less likely to communicate than the writer, regardless of air voice, who is intimately acquainted with the subject matter and knows what he's talking about. No announcer could have made "Deep Sorrow" as moving and communicative as McLendon did, because McLendon felt the words as he read what he had written.

EXAMPLES OF EDITORIALS

The subject matter and techniques of presentation by modern broadcasters are almost endless. While some licensees stick to bland, noncontroversial subjects, others fearlessly launch attacks against everything from local politicians to the heads of foreign governments. The National Association of Broadcasters' "Editorial Clearing House" supplies proof of some licensees' willingness to broadcast editorials that speak plainly of current events. KFI in Los Angeles directed this editorial against a state senator:

> Senator James Whetmore of Buena Park has said he would like reaction both from the public and the news media toward his possible introduction of legislation which would stipulate minimum educational standards or licensing procedures for California news reporters and broadcasters.
> Okay, Senator...KFI is happy to answer your request. Simply put, we're against either idea. Insofar as education is concerned, KFI's news staff is comprised both of those who possess college degrees and those who simply have graduated from high school. One thing all have, however, is a marked degree of expertise in expressing themselves...and of curiosity and interest in the world about them.
> We feel this is all they need.
> As to the licensing idea, Senator, it seems to KFI that this poses a very real danger of becoming the thin end of a wedge that easily could lead to government control of media...regardless of what beneficial reasons the author of such legislation might have.
> Now then, Senator Whetmore...if you were to suggest certain educational and licensing requirements that must be met before an individual could become a state legislator...

While the last paragraph of the editorial put tongue in cheek, it was a hardy rebuke to a politician who was attempting to increase government's hold on mass communications. In recent years, many broadcasters have become bolder in criticizing government and government officials. Gordon McLendon broadcast the following editorial in January, 1970:

Impeach Justice Douglas?

A few weeks back, when the nomination of Judge Clement Haynsworth to the Supreme Court was still hanging fire in the Senate, the New York **Daily News** delivered itself of an editorial that, to us, was a direct hit. The **Daily News** said at that time, quote:

"So a group of House members talks purposefully of impeaching Associate Justice William O. Douglas if the Senate rejects Haynsworth on ethical grounds."

But, said the **Daily News** back then, why wait? Why not bring impeachment proceedings against Douglas now? Douglas has been asking for it for years, and long ago, we feel, outlived any usefulness he may once have had on the high bench. Why wink at his rather frequently unethical conduct any longer? asks the **Daily News**.

Amen.

In March, 1972, WAZK (FM), billing itself as the "Ethnic Voice of Cleveland," editorially attacked the Federal Trade Commission. The editorial said in part:

The Federal Trade Commission is proposing that free air time be given to those who wish to challenge the claims made in radio and television commercials.

It doesn't tax the imagination at all to see how such a regulation would utterly destroy the advertiser supported system of broadcasting that has served America for more than four decades. On its merits, the FTC proposal hardly deserves consideration. The Trade Commission is charged by law with responsibility for policing advertising and it is shamelessly attempting to pass the buck to broadcasters. The proposal should promptly be assigned to the scrap heap of other bureaucratic crack-brained ideas.

In January, 1972, WPFB of Middletown, Ohio, took a crack at the local newspaper, the Middletown Journal.

"Wasn't that an interesting survey the Middletown Journal published in last Thursday's paper? But like all surveys, it's most important that you carefully interpret the questions. For instance...let's take just one question that was asked:

Quote: Suppose there is some news that you are very much interested in. Where would you be most likely to find out all there is about it?—end quote. First of all, the first part of this question reveals that you **already** know about it before you get to a newspaper. And in the second part of that question, the clue is...**all there is about it**. There's no doubt that the newspaper will give you detail after detail...but, chances are, you heard about it **first** on radio...with all the facts, not necessarily all the details. For example: When the Russians invaded Czechoslovakia, a study showed over 42 percent heard about it first on radio, 24 percent on TV, and 22 percent through newspapers. Even more impressive...when Jackie Kennedy made her epic announcement back in 1968...52 percent of the males 18 and over heard it on the radio...while only 9.3 percent read it in the newspapers.

There's an old saying...when you hear it, it's news...when you read it, it's history. And there's one more point: When was the last time you heard of an "extra?"

In May, 1972, KIRO Radio and Television in Seattle aired a strong editorial about what the writer termed "flimflam" journalism.

"That credibility gap" mantle that the press is so fond of hanging on the federal government may come home to roost. Pollster Louis Harris recently told the American Newspaper Publishers Association that the stature of newspapers has been dropping in the eyes of their readers. He said that those with "a great deal of respect" for newspapers dropped from 26 percent in 1968 to 18 percent in his latest survey. And even more to the point, those with "hardly any respect" jumped from 17 percent to 26 percent. Now, we're sure every newspaper reader can tell you why he thinks this is true. But we can't help but wonder if it isn't ordinarily a result of what some call "advocacy journalism" and others simply call slanted news. Years ago in journalism schools, they called it "subjective reporting" as opposed to "objective reporting." They taught it was wrong to mix editorial opinion with the professional reporting of news. But that was years ago. Now, there's a school of thought that a newsman should be an advocate...that, if he believes in a cause, he should be able to champion that cause as he reports the news. And the result? Pollster Harris said it...the stature of newspapers has been sharply declining in the eyes of their readers. And we suspect television viewers are just as critical. We think the people are becoming increasingly aware of "flimflam" journalism...twisting facts to influence the public in news reporting.

In December, 1971, WSAU Radio in Wausau, Wisconsin, broadcast a critique of federal bureaucracies in general and an FCC member in particular. The editorial said in part:

> Two years ago a member of the Federal Communications Commission urged that the so-called "Fairness Doctrine," which is supposed to insure balanced radio and television programing, be used against newspapers as well as the electronic media. In an August, 1969, speech in Dallas, Kenneth Cox of the FCC said, and we quote, "Congress could constitutionally apply counterparts of our equal-time and rights-of-reply obligations to most newspapers, since they move in, or clearly affect interstate commerce, and since the public interest in their providing their readers with both sides of important questions is clear."
>
> Such an attitude should clearly indicate that the bureaucrats are motivated by the old adage: "Give 'em an inch, and they'll take a mile."

In January, 1972, KSL (AM-FM-TV) in Salt Lake City delivered this well written editorial on "freedom of the press." The Justice Hugo Black quote in the last paragraph is particularly significant.

> Three cases are due to be argued before the U.S. Supreme Court in the next few weeks. The way these cases are decided will have enormous impact on the lives of

every American. Unfortunately, that impact will be little noticed because it will be largely invisible, whichever way these cases are decided.

They all involve newsmen who were challenged by subpoena to provide grand juries with information. All three declined on constitutional grounds. In one case, the court of appeals upheld the newsman, saying "the news media...should be free to pursue their own investigations without fear of governmental interferences and they should be able to protect their investigative processes."

It is understandable that some would wish to place curbs on the media. Television, radio, print—all are guilty of error. Almost all of this is due to the pressures of time and space and to the human element. The press is powerful, but it is owned and controlled by many very diverse persons and interests, and in the American tradition, it is competitive. If its product is unacceptable, it will not survive.

The most somber fact to bring to this consideration is that it is government and the power of government which in our own lifetimes is growing relentlessly. The danger which many see is that government will control all the essential functions of society before very long. The first step in that grim journey is control of the press.

As the late Justice Hugo Black, referring to the constitution, wrote in his last opinion: "The press was to serve the governed, not the governors. The government's power to censor the press was abolished so that the press would remain forever free to censure the government."

Station KWNO in Winona, Minnesota, is an example of a small-market station that editorializes regularly and even uses some production techniques that dramatize the introduction:

(Introduction)

KWNO speaks its mind (musical sting). This is an editorial feature of KWNO Radio—Pat Ellis speaking.

(Editorial)

Lately our government has been doing a great deal of talking about truth-in-advertising. We strongly urge them to put their own house in order first. How about a little more truth in government? The Pentagon and Anderson Papers clearly indicate that top officials do not hesitate to deceive whenever it suits them. KWNO agrees with truth-in-advertising. But we also feel a little more truth in government certainly wouldn't hurt. All that seems to be involved in this governmental deceit is the ability to not only admit failure but to learn from it and go on. This isn't a bad measure for government, either.

(Close)

This has been an editorial feature of KWNO.

In Tampa, Florida, WTVT Television became involved in a local controversy concerning abortions. The station took the position that government should not control abortions. This is how WTVT handled the rebuttal:

DR. MORONEY REPLIES AGAINST ABORTIONS

Last week a Channel 13 editorial suggested Florida lawmakers face up to the basic issue of whether or not government should control abortions, and suggested the decision would be that it shouldn't. In keeping with our policy of fairness, we hear tonight from Dr. John Moroney, speaking for the Florida Right-to-Life Committee.

(Run film for 3:00)

"The issue of abortion has become a very emotional one. We are sympathetic with the concerns of some of those who favor abortion. Channel 13 says we should face the issue squarely and we agree. Where we disagree is, what is the real basic issue here. The question is: **Does anyone have the right to deny life!**—the basic of all guaranteed rights to a living human? There are those who claim that the fetus is nothing more than a glob or a parasite, but it **is** alive and it **is** human. The product of human conception is alive because it has the ability to reproduce dying cells and it is human because, with nothing more than time and nutrition, it becomes one of us. I have never seen a human being conceive and deliver a dog or a flower. She always produces another human.

There is nothing magic that happens suddenly at 10 or 12 or 20 weeks that makes it human when it wasn't before.

"Channel 13 mentions cases of rape and incest. Let me put to rest once and for all the myth that most abortions are performed for these reasons. Only a very minor percentage of abortions being performed in New York are done for alleged rape. Certainly, we condemn rape and incest and sympathize with its victims. It is not the innocent baby, however, who is to blame or should be punished.

"Channel 13 suggests mental health and potential suicide as legitimate reasons for abortion. The American Journal of Obstetrics and Gynecology, January 15, 1968, states that actual suicides are four times greater among the general female population than among pregnant women.

"Since the life of a third innocent party is involved here, we believe that the state has the right and duty to protect that right to life. Abortion is a very negative approach to solving our problems, and it isn't negative approaches that have made this country great. Much must be done to better our lives and the lives of all of our citizens, but denying certain of those citizens the right to life, once they are conceived, regardless of how lofty the motives, is not the answer.

"Thank you."

(End film)

McLendon editorials are noted for their "last-line hookers," a sting, a rebuke, sarcasm, and sometimes humor. While he personally deals mainly with subjects of national and international interests and broadcasts his editorials on all McLendon Stations, his local managers are charged with the responsibility of providing editorials on local issues. In criticizing the welfare program in New York City, McLendon ended his editorial: "Well, after all is said and done, the Indians may have gotten the best of the Manhattan bargain. It might be financially prudent just to give it back to them."

In commenting on bureaucratic red tape, he said, "But ask the bureaucrats to show us how to simplify anything? That's like asking George Armstrong Custer to show us how to fight Indians."

On criticizing the ROTC: "Opposing the ROTC because you hate war is like opposing the fire department because you hate fires."

On Senator J. William Fulbright and equal time: "The senator's resolution now did not make it clear which of the many congressional performers will star in the Capitol television spectaculars, if the idea is forced on network television broadcasters. However, Senator Fulbright may have somebody in mind for the leading role. And we have a good idea who it is."

On women's rights in Russia: "Stalin granted men zero rights and granted women an exactly equal number of rights—zero. Stalin's dictatorship did many things to the Russian people, but one thing it did not do to any of them is to liberate them."

On the IRS revoking tax-exempt status of the Jerry Rubin Foundation: "That will make millions of Americans feel a little better on April 15. Not a lot better, but a little better."

On satellite countries: "The Russians 'consult' with their satellite in just about the same way that a ventriloquist consults with his dummy."

On Rockefeller's welfare plan for New York: "Governor Rockefeller thinks this shyness about showing up to pick up welfare checks indicates the state of New York was being chiseled. Could be, governor, could be."

On Lyndon Johnson: "Mr. Johnson seems, as always, to speak in terms of high idealism. It is just that, as usual, we cannot understand what he is talking about. We is a simple country boy."

On J. Edgar Hoover critics: "Since the suspicious Mr. Hoover turned out to be right and his critics wrong, you'd think they'd pay him an apology, wouldn't you? If so, think again."

MAILING BROADCAST EDITORIALS

Most stations that editorialize use an editorial "letterhead" in sending copies to interested parties. Station WITI in Milwaukee uses this approach, and includes as part of the letterhead an offer of response time.

"WITI-TV offers a reasonable opportunity to reply to the views expressed in this editorial to a responsible person or group representing a significant opposing viewpoint, provided written request for reply time is submitted to WITI-TV within one week of this broadcast. Copies of this editorial are available upon written request. Indicate copies desired."

While it is doubtful that WITI's "one week" rule would hold up under a serious challenger, the station should be commended for accepting responsibility for offering reply time instead of leaning on requirements of the FCC's Fairness Doctrine. Station WTOP in Washington, D.C., employs the following language on its editorial letterhead:

"Our editorial policy is to assist our audience in better understanding public issues. We welcome comments on our editorials and recognize our obligation to present contrasting points of view from responsible spokesmen. We reserve the right to designate spokesmen and to deny such requests if we believe that the viewpoint has been fairly represented or the issue is not a controversial subject of public importance. This editorial, or any part thereof, may be reproduced only with proper credit for WTOP Radio and WTOP-TV."

PRODUCTION TECHNIQUES

It is apparent that several TV operations around the country use some extraordinary production techniques. Radio station licensees seem to prefer a straight "message" approach. Station WITI-TV in Milwaukee "produced" this editorial in January, 1972:

STUDENTS SEEK CHANGE THROUGH SYSTEM

VIDEO	AUDIO
Camera on Zimmerman:	There's a changed attitude on our college campuses these days. As a recent Associated Press survey found, the radical leaders have left...and students are making a greater effort to effect change within the system.
Film: Demonstration on campus:	The long, trying period of violence and confrontation appears to be virtually ended. The questions naturally arise: Are today's students less interested in bringing about change? Have they become apathetic? Are they no longer interested in correcting inequities in today's world?
Camera on Zimmerman:	We don't think so. It seems that our students changed their approach at about the time of the Sterling Hall bombing on the Madison campus...that senseless, useless killing of a young graduate student...in August of 1970. Perhaps it was this tragedy that provided a sobering influence among young people...not only in Wisconsin but around the nation. To some indefinable degree, it served to tell them that violence doesn't work...it doesn't bring change...in fact, might retard the changes they desire.

	There were other contributing factors. The lowering of the voting age to 18 told our young people that their elders want their participation in planning for the future. The vote gave them a stake in the whole democratic process...a precious right they didn't have before.
Film: Students on campus:	TV6 hopes that the disruption, the violence of past years is gone...and gone forever. Youth still has its ideals about the morality of war...its abhorrence of poverty and corruption where it exists today.
Camera on Zimmerman:	We believe that the majority of students...those who want change, but want it accomplished effectively through participation in the democratic system...are finally prevailing.

WCBS-TV in New York employed slides in this presentation:

Thomas Jefferson warned that for democracy to work, it was necessary to "illuminate the minds of the people..." The recent joint appearances of Senators Humphrey and McGovern on CBS' "Face the Nation" (slide Humphrey and McGovern on "Face the Nation") and NBC's "Meet the Press" (slide Humphrey and McGovern on "Meet the Press") helped to "illuminate the minds of the people" in a way Jefferson might have liked, because they dealt with issues. Voters were able to watch the two leading Democratic contenders discuss tax and welfare reform, income redistribution, defense spending, and the war in Vietnam.

But as useful as these broadcasts were, it looks as if such head-to-head confrontations aren't likely to happen soon again. Because, although at first these news interview broadcasts had been exempt from the "equal-time" rule requiring television stations to give all candidates for the same office an equivalent amount of time, a federal court changed the picture, ruling that candidate Shirley Chisholm had to be granted equal time.

Apparently because of this decision, the third scheduled appearance of the candidates on ABC's "Issues and Answers" (slides showing five candidates on "Issues and Answers") ended up with a cast of five instead of two, as originally planned, featuring not only Senators McGovern and Humphrey, but also Mayor Sam Yorty and a representative of Governor George Wallace in California, as well as Representative Chisholm, separately, in New York.

The result was that the issues, so well defined on the previous occasions, were diluted. And with five contenders in the ring, it was hard to tell who was landing punches and who was pulling them. It was obvious that two's a confrontation—five's a crowd.

While formats may be worked out for major candidates to appear together, with other time periods granted to minor candidates—the federal court ruling discourages this from happening. For the ruling has created an atmosphere of confusion and uncertainty about the ways broadcasters can provide information to the voters. And this uncertainty will persist until the "equal-time" rule is lifted.

That's why we urge Congress to act to remove the "equal-time" restriction. More than ever, we believe that in 1972, with fundamental issues and sharp differences between candidates emerging, there should be nationally televised debates between the major party candidates. We think Jefferson would have wanted it that way.

No radio stations included in this study indicated extensive use of production techniques. Certainly, each licensee should judge for himself whether such devices will benefit or hurt his editorial effort. But Sol Taishoff of **Broadcasting** magazine was entirely correct in saying that radio editorials need not be dull or "straight" to communicate believable ideas and information. This hypothetical example is offered as a possible approach.

OURTOWN

VOICER ON MAYOR:

And if I am elected Mayor of Ourtown you may rest assured that my administration will move immediately to provide better and more efficient services to our citizens. (FADE after 3 seconds of applause for:)

EDITORIALIST:

That was Mayor John Stumpp speaking at a political rally during his campaign for mayor last year. His promises to provide better and more efficient services have not been kept. KXXX went to the people last week to find out how some promises have not been kept.

VOICER MONTAGE:

"I'm Mrs. George Bennett and I believe our garbage service has gotten worse since Mayor Stumpp was elected." "I'm Bob Cody and I used to ride the bus to work. But since the city took the bus company over, I've been unable to depend on it."

EDITORIALIST:

And so on...KXXX talked with dozens of citizens directly affected by the mayor's failure to keep his promises.

VOICER ON MAYOR:

"You may rest assured that my administration will move immediately" (FADE FOR:)

EDITORIALIST:

Yes, Mayor Stumpp. You promised to move immediately. When, pray tell, is immediately?

Aside from voicers, radio editorials could be punctuated with appropriate music and sound effects. There is always the danger of overdramatization and losing the believability of the opinion. But used in moderation and in a highly discriminatory fashion, radio editorials could be made more effective through the use of music, sound, and actualities. The idea of making them as aurally attractive as commercials lacks appeal, but certainly most licensees have the imagination and wherewithal to eliminate the blandness that plagues most radio editorials. But just as the newspaper publisher should not discontinue editorializing because he doesn't have an attractive typeface, neither should the broadcaster stop editorializing because he doesn't have the time or the means to produce the editorial. It is better to editorialize dully than not to editorialize at all.

EDITORIAL CAMPAIGNS

Often, a station resorts to a series of editorials when management believes it cannot make its point with a single effort. Sometimes, these develop into campaigns that extend for several weeks and involve elaborate production and research. Station WGN-TV's Bob Manewith provided an example of an editorial series on "The Future of Education," and an example of a campaign entitled "Anti-Drug Abuse Week."

THE FUTURE OF EDUCATION—NO. 1

Public education in the United States is in the midst of great change...much of what has happened already has been the result of court orders. Much of what will happen will be the result of the program submitted to congress by President Nixon on March 17th. Much of what has happened, however, could have been avoided, had state legislatures and local school boards taken initiatives before school problems found their way into the courts.

Unfortunately, emotion has muddied the waters. The emotion is reaction to a court order which says that busing white children to black communities and black children to white communities is a suitable tool for ending segregation in public schools.

The historic 1954 decision banning legal school segregation was based on the belief that separate but supposedly equal facilities did not bring equal education. This order was directed at the states and school districts which had, under law, maintained separate school systems for blacks and whites.

Still unresolved is the question of school districts and local schools which are all black or all white, or close to either, not by law, but because of housing patterns or other circumstances. Also unresolved, at least for the present, is the disparity of education from community to community, based on the community's ability to pay for education.

Busing, for its own sake, is **not** the ultimate solution, not the way to bring integration to schools, and not the way to provide an equal education, a quality education, to everyone. Busing, however, can become the emotional confuser, the muddier.

This nation cannot afford to maintain unequal education, whatever its cause. We cannot let the emotionalism of the busing issue keep us from resolving this crisis in education.

No. 2

Resolving the future of education...of gaining an equal and quality education for everyone...has been confused by the emotional issue of busing. We have stated, in another editorial, that busing for its own sake, to put white children and black children together in the same school, provides no insurance that either group will benefit educationally.

The real answer is an equal education for everyone, regardless of where the schoolhouse is located, regardless of whether the children are of one background or of many. We also feel that "equal" does NOT mean bringing the education down from its upper levels or averaging the level between the so-called best and worst schools. It means, it **must** mean, bringing the level of education for all schools up to the level of the best schools.

This can't be done overnight and it can't be done without money. First, congress must recognize, as the Administration already has, that this is a crisis and provide the funds to raise education levels. Second, the states must take the major role in financing public education, so that once a level of quality equality has been reached, its maintenance will be assured.

On the national level, proposals are pending in congress. On the state level, we can expect introduction of several programs when the General Assembly reconvenes on April 12th. Our lawmakers, both in Springfield and Washington, have to recognize the urgency and act.

No. 3

The 1954 Supreme Court decision, which ordered an end to legal segregation in public schools, saw some northern liberals delight as southerners struggled to undo the traditions and habits of nearly a century. Now, there is some reversal of roles, with the courts holding that even though schools in the North have not been segregated by law...they are still segregated. And, say the courts, as long as they are segregated, education is not equal.

According to some southerners, court-ordered busing will teach formerly smug northerners a lesson. Perhaps it will; but if it does, it is the wrong lesson. Busing can teach only that black children and white children can be placed in the same school. It cannot guarantee that being together will improve the education of either group, which is what it should do.

If there is a benefit in integration, that benefit cannot be realized in the piecemeal approach of busing. True integration requires true and unrestricted open housing, the open housing of economic choice and ability...not the movement of hundreds and thousands of children from one area to another for a quarter of each day.

Quality education, and equality in education, are what we need. If integrated schools are necessary to that goal, then true integration...not the quarterday of the bus...is also necessary. Integration can be achieved with moving vans...not with buses.

An editorial critic might object to the overuse of the phrase "much of" in the opening paragraph of No. 1. But if the repetition fitted the style of the person reading the material, it would add to the clarity of the presentation. A great number of ideas are presented in the series. And the editorials obviously were the result of extensive research by a skilled writer working for an organization that could afford to pay such talent.

The campaign waged by WGN Continental is among the more extensive conducted in the nation. The following report was prepared by or under the direction of Editorial Director Bob Manewith and submitted to the Illinois Crime Investigating Commission. The report could also be used to support claims to the Federal Communications Commission that WGN has contributed to the solution of Chicago's most pressing problems.

NARCOTICS AND DANGEROUS DRUG PROBLEMS

In the process of ascertaining community problems and community needs, WGN placed top priority on the drug abuse problem among youth many months ago, and during 1970 conducted three major campaigns on the subject. These special, exclusive efforts by our stations were in addition to the substantial support we gave to the industry-wide "Straight Dope," National Institute for Mental Health and Department of Health, Education and Welfare campaigns.

Brief summaries of these 1970 campaigns follow.

April 26-May 3, 1970

During this period, WGN Television presented a concentrated eight-day all-out alert campaign to warn those individuals, especially the youth of the community contemplating the use of drugs, of the inherent potential dangers of "turning on."

To formulate sound plans for this concentrated effort, the management of WGN met prior to the campaign with representatives of medical, educational, and governmental organizations and agencies involved in the narcotics program. In addition to a saturation schedule of announcements, we addressed various aspects of the subject in daily interviews, discussion programs and on-the-scene news features. Among the programs involved were the "Tim Conway Show," "Your Right To Say It," "People to People," "The David Susskind Show," and "The Cromie Circle." We also presented a series of guest editorials by:

115

Hubert H. Humphrey, former vice president of the United States;

Thomas A. Foran, U.S. district attorney;

Kenneth Blumenthal, Trustee, Key Club International;

Dr. Ernest Breed, President, Illinois State Medical Association;

Ernie Banks, Chicago Cubs;

Mitchell Ware, Director, Illinois Bureau of Investigation;

Judge Kenneth Wendt, Cook County Circuit Court.

Literature on the subject was offered to the public free of charge.

June 1970

WGN Radio, participating in a combined effort of Illinois broadcasters against drug abuse, presented a month-long program of special broadcasts, editorials, and messages by well known sports personalities. Every significant phase of the subject was reviewed and discussed in detail.

Messages and special features on the subject were incorporated in all of WGN Radio's top-rated programs, starting with the Wally Phillips Show and including the Roy Leonard, Eddie Hubbard, Howard Miller programs, and others. Special programs on the use and abuse of drugs were offered on "Extension 720," WGN Radio's two-hour discussion program hosted nightly by Dan Price.

Cold Turkey Isn't Something You Eat
September-October 1970

Because of the widespread and significant response to the two previous campaigns, which we felt had just scratched the surface of the insidious drug abuse problem, WGN Radio and WGN Television, in a joint effort, launched a dramatic extension of the effort with the beginning of the school year in September 1970.

The concept, plan, and creative materials were produced by WGN Continental's advertising agency, Foote, Cone & Belding, working in cooperation with WGN's program, public affairs, public relations, and advertising departments.

"Cold Turkey Isn't Something You Eat" was the blunt and provocative theme of this extensive joint effort; and the expression "Cold Turkey" has become the trademark of this hard-hitting campaign from coast to coast and in many foreign countries.

For the Chicagoland area served by WGN Radio and WGN Television, the campaign again involved all-out programing on the subject: saturation schedules of special announcements offering a free packet of literature to the public, interviews, discussions, special program features, and meaningful editorials.

This campaign was augmented with a series of four startling full-page advertisements that were placed in Chicago's four daily newspapers, with single insertions in several other publications in the area (Commerce Magazine, Chicago Magazine, The Chicago Defender, etc.).

The campaign was also supplemented by a series of three dramatic posters designed for display in gathering places for young people. A total of more than 350 poster sets were distributed through YMCA and other youth-oriented organizations, and in response to requests from schools, teachers, and students.

The response to this final 1970 effort has been so overwhelming that we had to reprint the literature and posters for free distribution twice.

Although the on-the-air and newspaper campaigns were concluded by November 1, we are still receiving several hundred requests each week for free packets of literature, and a continuing demand for the posters from schools and other organizations concerned with youth has been generated by their display throughout the area.

More than 40,000 individual packets of literature will be distributed to parents and other concerned citizens in the area by the end of the year. More than 1500 sets of posters have been distributed for display in places where young people gather. More than 200 requests have been received from various city, county, and state organizations and agencies, as well as private business companies in Illinois.

Thirteen other radio and television stations and 19 newspaper publishers in Illinois have requested the creative materials (see "Cold Turkey" Nationwide) to enable them to sponsor and conduct local "Cold Turkey" campaigns in their communities.

"Cold Turkey" Nationwide

Impressed with the candid, dramatic creative materials (newspaper advertisements, posters, etc.) produced for this campaign, WGN Continental, at the suggestion of Foote, Cone & Belding, offered them free of charge to other broadcasters and newspaper publishers throughout the United States.

The WGN Continental offer was made in a special advertisement placed in many business publications (Broadcasting, Advertising Age, Editor & Publisher, Variety, Television-Radio Age) and in the New York Times, Washington Post, and the Los Angeles Times.

The kit of campaign materials was designed to enable other communicators to sponsor a "Cold Turkey" program in their own communities. Included in the kit:

(1) Proofs of the four print advertisements
(2) A sample of each of three posters
(3) A sample "Cold Turkey" packet of literature
(4) Suggested text for radio announcements
(5) Suggested text for television announcements
(6) Suggestions on how to conduct a "Cold Turkey" campaign in any community.

We expected (and hoped) to get about 100 responses to this offer. To date we have filled more than 3000 orders and they are still coming in every week, although the offer was last made more than two months ago.

The requests have come from all of the 50 states in the Union and 21 foreign countries. More than 1000 other broadcasters and newspaper publishers have sent for the creative materials, expressing an interest and willingness to conduct campaigns in their local communities.

And significantly, the balance of the requests have come from a wide variety of private business enterprises (other than broadcasters or publishers), national, state, county, and local agencies and organizations, educational and religious institutions, and—in many cases—just concerned citizens.

This all leads us to the following conclusions:

1. The response to our campaigns has indicated a substantial need for more readily available facilities and professional referral services to accommodate those who are attempting to fight drug abuse as a personal problem or those who are trying to cope with it in their families or among their friends.

2. The tremendous response to the WGN Continental offer in business publications indicates a substantial concern with drug abuse as an employee problem by business firms. This suggests further study of the problem by the business community.

3. Our campaigns have demonstrated a tremendous concern about drug abuse by parents and those individuals and agencies involved in educating and guiding young people.

From the voluminous mail received, concern of young people themselves with the problem has also been very apparent. In many cases, young people have indicated a need to talk to someone about the temptation and the problem—and preferably to their parents.

4. Our campaigns have also received a surprisingly big response from free-enterprise business companies seeking not only to learn more about the problem and its roots but also volunteering to do something about the problem not only in their companies but in their communities.

5. We are making some progress and are now in a healthier position than we were a year ago because the problem has been brought out into the open, is now being fully discussed in the public forums that radio, television, and other media provide. There is now an important and significant exchange of dialog in public media and this is bound to rub off to some meaningful degree in the important parent-child relationship.

6. Broadcasting is playing an important leading role. Because of the intimacy of radio and television, they are in

a position to be most effective and especially with the young people.

We have encouraged frank discussion of drugs and the problems caused by drugs between parents and their children—not just about drugs, per se, but also the reasons why they are being misused. In the WGN Radio and WGN Television campaigns, we have stressed to parents and young people alike the basic need for being knowledgeable on the subject and toward that end have distributed free of charge to the public thousands (40,000-plus) of packets of literature on the subject.

7. There are many examples of broadcasters recognizing and attacking this problem as a volunteer public service. Another noteworthy example in this state—in addition to the WGN effort—has been WBBM Radio's "Dead End Trips, Drug Abuse in Illinois" campaign in which more than 100 stations in Illinois participated.

Radio broadcasters throughout the State of Illinois responded unanimously to Governor Ogilvie's proclamation designating June as Radio Broadcasters Against Drug Abuse Month, a campaign to communicate the truth about drug abuse and its dangers to the youth of this state.

8. Is what we are doing effective? A tough one to answer, but we do feel that the antismoking situation provides a relevant parallel. Adults are well aware today of the obvious impact antismoking announcements on television and radio have had—especially the impact on young people. We feel that broadcasting—if we hit the subject consistently, frankly, candidly, dramatically—may exert a similar significant and profound effect.

CHAPTER 8

Editorial Practices

It would take years of correspondence and research to determine with precision the ends to which broadcasters go to editorialize or not editorialize. And it would be fallacious to study and publish reports on those who avoid editorializing for whatever reasons. Considering the alternatives, it seemed appropriate to seek out information on stations from every major region of the nation and prepare narratives on their editorial policies and procedures. Some licensees have definitive policies that demand of management a consistent editorial effort. Others have policies that simply state that editorials will be carried when appropriate.

Stations studied in this text are located throughout the country. Care was taken to peruse non-newspaper-owned stations as well as those with newspaper affiliation where editorial policy may or may not be set by the publisher-licensee. Network-owned and -operated efforts were given particular attention, as some of the best editorials were found at those stations.

However, the study developed adequate proof that to editorialize effectively and conscientiously, a station need not be a WMAQ-TV in Chicago or a WMCA Radio in New York. Small stations such as KMAR in Winnsboro, Louisiana, have aggressive editorial policies that are just as important to local citizens as William Allen White's magnificent effort was to his readers in rural Kansas.

Many stations that air editorials do not, in fact, editorialize as the term is commonly understood. Argument is not offered, offense is never intended, and little good is ever accomplished. But the same is true of many newspapers, weekly and daily, however little consolation this offers the advocate of stronger editorial efforts.

The National Association of Broadcasters, in the fall of 1966, conducted a mail survey of radio and television stations and found that about 55 percent were broadcasting editorials. One out of three stations responding had never editorialized. About 10 percent used to editorialize, but had discontinued it for various reasons. The NAB learned that the most active editorializers, like editorializing stations generally, were found among the larger broadcast operations. Gross revenues were illustrative: of the editorializing radio stations grossing $500,000 or more yearly, 57 percent editorialized about at least five new subjects each month. Only one-third of the radio stations reporting annual revenues below $250,000 covered this wide a range of subject matter. And the same relationship was found in the case of television: the more affluent the station, the greater the diversity of topics covered.

WMCA, NEW YORK

R. Peter Straus, president of Straus Communications, Inc., licensee of WMCA (AM) in New York City, said that radio and television stations should be free to express licensee views on matters of importance to the community served, "whether the issue be a Presidential endorsement or a badly maintained playground." In the period preceding the Mayflower Decision in 1941, and for eight or nine years afterward, radio stations were forbidden to editorialize. Mr. Straus' father, Nathan Straus, chafed at the absurdity of the ban.

"He could, he felt, employ a commentator to disseminate his views, but he was prohibited from broadcasting them himself," the younger Mr. Straus recalled. "Now that broadcasters are allowed and indeed encouraged to editorialize, our policy has not changed. We believe licensees should editorialize."

When the idea of a textbook on broadcast editorializing was first mentioned to Gordon McLendon, the pioneer radio licensee immediately suggested the work of "Peter Straus must be included in any work dealing with the subject." WMCA's almost unbelievable struggle for equal representation in New York State is now a matter of historical record. It was a case of a citizen, who also happened to be licensee of a radio station, using every available resource, including his radio station, money, and personal connections, to correct a condition he thought inimical to the democracy of his community.

In this situation, Straus obviously thought first of correcting what he believed to be an unfair, inequitable system of representation in the New York Legislature. Station WMCA was to be only one weapon employed in a nearly four-year fight to bring the state under the "one man, one vote" concept of representation. Straus' idea of public service is an admirable one that seems to parallel that of some of the great publishers such as William Allen White, Joseph Pulitzer, George Bannerman Dealy, and scores of other, lesser known, newspapermen who put the public's welfare ahead of profit and self-aggrandizement.

Straus' policy of broadcasting editorials that "take strong positions and suggest actions that the community can take..." has been exemplified by campaigns to lower the voting age to 18, dislodge the slum landlords of New York City, and make his city a separate state of the Union. Compare these blockbuster editorial efforts to those of the neckless licensee who fearlessly criticizes a group of out-of-town high school football fans whose conduct lacked decorum in last night's at-home game.

In spite of strong, thought-provoking editorials, Straus said he knows of few propositions that are harder to prove than a contention that a given editorial has positive results. "We editorialized repeatedly about state legislative reapportionment, but we also went to court to fight malapportionment. We helped provide evidence to indict slum landlords, but we also helped draft legislation to make it harder for them to hide behind corporate fronts.

"We've campaigned for lowering the voting age to 18, but we can claim only a small share of the credit for the constitutional amendment that made that a reality. We've also campaigned to make New York City a separate state, and while the campaign has not yet succeeded, we think one positive result is that New Yorkers are a lot more conscious of the various ways in which the state discriminates against the city."

With regard to the unique idea that New York City become a city-state (as in Athens of Attica), Straus, on June 7-8, 1971, ran the following editorial:

> To some people, the idea of New York City becoming a separate state is still a joke. But after what happened to the city at this year's legislative session in Albany, it's just not a laughing matter any more.
> Now, carving a city-state out of the Empire state won't be easy. For one thing, it can't be done without Albany's approval, and eventually congress has to get into the act, too.
> But we think it's time to stop talking about the obstacles and start working to overcome them. And we think the way to do that is with a referendum here in the city on whether or not to become a state.
> We've already done a little research on the subject, and it seems to us that there are several ways to get that question on the ballot in the city this November. We don't really care which one the city uses. But we do care that the voters of New York City should get a chance this year to tell Albany to shape up—or we'll check out.

Most of WMCA's editorials are brief, written in the simplest possible language, and are broadcast with a calm but forceful delivery that reflects the perspicacity of the licensee. An editorial doesn't have to emote to be effective; sound effects are not required to dramatize the editorial's essential points. This is not to say that emotionalism and dramatization are needless, wasted tools, for they are not. But there are times when simple, unadulterated candor is more appropriate. The Straus technique is to broadcast editorials in series, with each element of the series dwelling on a single point of the whole idea. This procedure is used in commercial announcements, actually, because of the average listener's inability to absorb and deal with more than a single idea. Station WMCA broadcasts each editorial from four to eight times daily during a one- or two-day stretch. Each station studied in this text may have a different idea on scheduling, much as an advertiser will perceive different tactics for airing commercials.

The WMCA effort on redistricting New York State is probably the most colossal effort on record of a licensee effort to make changes in the community of license. Over a four-year period, here is the chronology of activity:

January, 1961—(a) Max Gross, former New York City councilman, long associated with reform and welfare issues, urges Peter Straus and WMCA to resort to court action to overturn New York apportionment.

January, 1961—(b) Straus contacts attorney Leonard Sand, Straus' brother-in-law and counsel for WMCA, and asks him to examine the feasibility of a lawsuit.

May 1, 1961—Station WMCA goes to federal district court challenging New York apportionment on grounds it violated the Equal Protection Clause of the Fourteenth Amendment by giving the more populous areas fewer representatives than their number warranted. On May 2, 1961, Peter Straus went on the air with the following editorial:

> There are 25 counties in upstate New York which, taken together, have barely a third the population of Brooklyn, but they cast more votes than Brooklyn in the New York State Assembly.
> Why? Because seats in both houses of the New York State Legislature are assigned throughout the state under a formula which favors upstate New York over New York City.
> WMCA is doing something about it. This week WMCA filed a suit in federal court aimed at winning more equal representation for all voters in the state.
> If you would like to join the fight, send a card to Equal Vote, WMCA, New York 17. That's Equal Vote, WMCA, New York 17. Give **your** support to this campaign to make **your** vote as good as the vote of New Yorkers upstate.

(This particular editorial is a product of WMCA's policy to take strong positions and suggest community action.)

Later in May, Straus ran another editorial pointing out again that upstate citizens had more clout at the state capital than their fellow citizens in the more populous New York City. The same idea was used, but the second editorial compared Schuyler County (with 15,000 residents) with a NYC assembly district (with 110,000 residents). The chronology continues:

July 7, 1961—District court judge orders the convening of a three-judge panel to hear WMCA's case.

January 11, 1962—Three-judge court rejects WMCA arguments.

February 5, 1962—WMCA appeals directly to U.S. Supreme Court.

The defeat at the hands of the three-judge court set WMCA back only briefly. After filing the appeal with the Supreme Court, Straus took to the air again with new information on the struggle:

> Two years ago, the famous Peck Commission received a damning report on how the state cheats New York City out of its fair share of seats in the legislature. That report, by Professor Ruth Silva, was so damning it's never been published. In fact, out of fear that the Peck Commission might follow up on it, the upstate barons who crack the whip in Albany even went so far as to abolish the commission itself.
> Today this very issue of your right to full representation in the legislature is before the U.S. Supreme Court in a case brought by WMCA. But meanwhile that report to the Peck Commission remains a state secret. How much longer will the facts be kept from the public?
> Well, I'll tell you how long. Until six o'clock tonight. That's when WMCA, having obtained the suppressed report, will make it public. You can hear the facts tonight on WMCA's six o'clock news. They've been swept under the rug long enough.

By this time in the campaign, Straus and WMCA had drawn fire from Governor Nelson Rockefeller and other state officials who opposed reapportionment. The subject was being discussed by virtually every newspaper and alert broadcast station in the state. The chronology continues:

June 11, 1962—The Supreme Court vacates the three-judge court's decision and remands the case to the lower court for a hearing on its merits.

August 1, 1962—The hearing begins.

August 16, 1962—Case dismissed on its merits.

At this point, Straus went on the air with:

> WMCA's lawyers advise us that we have strong grounds for another appeal to the Supreme Court. WMCA will make that appeal. We are in this battle to the end—a battle to make you a first-class citizen of New York State.

August 29, 1962—WMCA appeals again to the Supreme Court.

June 10, 1963—The Supreme Court announces "probable jurisdiction."

Straus had this to say on the air:

> WMCA and the voters of New York State are cheering today's call by the nation's chief umpire. In deciding to hear WMCA's case, the Supreme Court has given New Yorkers up and down the state another turn at bat. We may be home soon.
>
> Nelson Rockefeller, unfortunately, has yet to take his cuts against the unfair apportionment of New York's state legislature. Earlier this year, when one bill for apportionment reform was killed in committee, the citizens of his state heard not one word of complaint from Nelson Rockefeller. The governor seems to prefer the security of the dugout to real action against New York's legislative malapportionment.

In another editorial in August, Straus said:

> In our state assembly, Paul Taylor of Yates County represents barely a tenth as many voters as the average assemblyman from New York City.

That's exactly why WMCA has asked the U.S. Supreme Court to rule that the apportionment of our legislature violates your constitutional rights.

But upstate Assemblyman Taylor disagrees. "Civic virtue," he says, "lives in the country." By contrast, he implies, the big city breeds all kinds of Communists, killers, and nuts.

Now, the notion of virtue as a qualification for voting is interesting in a way. But it might be hard to prove that a roadside bookie in Yates County is ten times as virtuous as, say, Cardinal Spellman.

And it might be hard to explain why the legislative spokesman for our virtuous yeoman upstate makes an annual practice of stealing New York City blind when it comes to voting state aid.

If that's civic virtue, WMCA takes a stand for sin.

The chronology continues:

September, 1963—WMCA, now joined by New York City and Nassau County, filed briefs with the Supreme Court. (During this period, WMCA was joined in litigation by the American Civil Liberties Union, the American Jewish Congress, and the Legal Defense and Educational Fund of the NAACP.)

September 9, 1963—WMCA editorially acknowledges support from other litigants.

September 30, 1963—U.S. Department of Justice enters case on side of WMCA.

November 12-13, 1963—Case argued before Supreme Court.

While the Supreme Court considered the arguments, Straus kept the line tight with a barrage of editorials attacking Governor Rockefeller's alleged indifference to the needs of city residents. Straus pulled no punches, as this editorial indicates:

> The first rule of Republican politics is that a governor must have a balanced budget if he wants to run for

President. And so Governor Rockefeller just had to submit a balanced budget for New York.

First he wrapped up a bundle of tax and other gimmicks good for this year only. Then he did what comes naturally when money's tight in New York State: He swindled New York City.

Though the city has always gotten far less than its fair share of state aid, the governor now wants to cut us down some more.

And the victims hardest hit will be the kids in our public schools. Last year the state spent over a hundred dollars more on each school child upstate than it spent in the city. But this year the spread will be even greater.

That's what it's costing our children to help Nelson Rockefeller run for President.

The chronology continues:

June 15, 1964—The Supreme Court declared that the Equal Protection Clause requires that seats in a bicameral state legislature must be apportioned on a population basis.

And so that was the decision the proponents of reapportionment had awaited. Legislative and legal skirmishes continued into 1966, but WMCA had won its case. In subsequent years, the station contributed materially to the public's understanding of efforts to redraw city and congressional district lines for reapportionment purposes.

Dr. Calvin B. T. Lee, a staff associate with the American Council on Education in Washington, prepared a detailed chronology of events in the case that was published in 1967 by Charles Schribner's Sons, New York. Dr. Lee, a graduate of Columbia Law School and New York University Law School, addressed himself to the WMCA case, even though there were several other similar cases pending in the courts. He chose the New York litigation because, among other reasons, New York is the biggest and most complex state in the union and because the case "presents the unusual feature of a litigant—a radio station—influencing action by an aggressive publicity campaign, as well as by skillful courtroom advocacy." Dr. Lee said his study "reveals the influence of the communications media in the shaping of American political thought."

While no serious-minded editorialist could appreciate hearing his editorials regarded as "publicity" pieces, any licensee must agree with Dr. Lee that WMCA's part in such historic litigation was extraordinary if not unique. And perhaps Peter Straus was being modest when he said it was hard to prove that a "given editorial has positive results." Dr. Lee obviously saw it differently.

PAUL HARVEY, ABC CHICAGO

In the WMCA story, Peter Straus quoted his father, Nathan, as saying the FCC's ban on editorializing was absurd, that a licensee's views could be disseminated by a "commentator" but not by himself. Indeed, licensee views must have in many instances been expressed by commentators during the years when editorializing was forbidden, although it would appear near impossible to support such a generalization.

One of the few remaining nationally known commentators is Paul Harvey of the American Broadcasting Company. Mr. Harvey is successor or contemporary to such notables as Walter Winchell, Eric Sevareid, Quentin Reynolds, Gabriel Heatter, Edward R. Murrow, H. V. Kaltenborn, to arbitrarily select a few and define their work as "commentary." Reynolds, for example, was known primarily as a "news analyst," while Sevareid simply makes "observations" about the news. One of government's chief complaints about news media in the early 70s was the TV network newsmen's "instant analysis" of major political speeches. It was a matter of routine, for example, for the three majors to "explain" what the President had just "explained" in a national three-network appearance. Former Vice President Spiro Agnew, in particular, took exception to this practice.

There can be little doubt that broadcasters such as Winchell and Kaltenborn were commentators. That is, they reported the news and they said what they thought of the people and events named in the news. They reported editorially and analytically and with a candor and forcefulness matched only by such newspaper columnists as Jack Anderson, Carl Rowan, Drew Pearson, to name only a few.

Harvey bills himself as a "reporter"; but routinely he attacks, editorially, deep social problems such as those occasionally created by news libertines. Harvey's attack on the idea of "equal opportunity" illustrates:

WHO CARES WHAT JERRY RUBIN THINKS?

Who cares what Jerry Rubin thinks?

Pollsters are fascinated with what criminals think about prisons and what hooligans think about policemen and how undergraduates think a college should run...

What's the matter with us? We're listening for advice of the least responsible, least respectable, most disreputable malcontents!

Los Angeles called it "Pershing Square." Chicagoans called theirs "Bughouse Square." Every big city had some place for would-be reformers to sound off.

The traditional anarchists and the oddballs and the weirdos were allowed to attract a crowd by shouting derision at the establishment.

It was all right. It was a place for the chronic malcontents to ventilate their frustrations or satisfy their egos and the rest of us could stop by, if we wanted to, for amusement.

Some of their audiences, frustrated pensioners and kookie kids got their kicks from the daring name-calling.

But nowadays we are putting those nuts on nationwide TV!

Mostly, it's the insatiable appetite of the so-called "talk shows" or "interview programs" which focuses the limelight on homes, prostitutes, group sexpots, and charlatan crusaders.

Any griper on any subject is allowed a sympathetic hearing until, by the time they've made the rounds of the networks, their premise, however preposterous, begins to take on an aura of validity.

In the dear dead days, BTV, our nation upheld worthy heroes. Men and women of valor, of benefaction, of accomplishment...

Boys wanted to grow up to be like Tom Edison or Babe Ruth or Slim Lindberg...

Or they wanted to grow up to be Horatio Alger industrialists or locomotive engineers or tradesmen or policemen...

Now, yesterday's heroes are all battered voodoo dolls for unworthy, unproductive, unwashed hopheads to stick pins in.

And TV's talk shows are not their only forum. Today's front pages are wearing yesterday's unmentionables. Competing news media spotlight all manner of rogues and rascals and gutterbums and, however we might not mean to, elevate demagogues to prominence, solicit support for them...

In the good name of "tolerance" a bad **fool-osophy** has been created which presumes that anybody heretofore downtrodden should be allowed hereafter to get away with murder.

I believe this current cult of Satan-worship will subside. I believe today's enlightened young, having drunk deep from the polluted well of permissiveness and promiscuity and professional perfidy will not look to the dung pile for tomorrow's leaders.

Meanwhile, I would hope that we with the monumental responsibility for evaluating what's newsworthy will assist that end, will pray for more wisdom to recognize the unworthy and will exercise our option to look the other way.

Perhaps the most irreparable damage which we do is in focusing so much attention on the irrational, the exceptional, the malcontent, and the misfit that our young people see things as worse than they are; then, feeling the world is beyond repair, they despair.

If page one is unfair—if page one distorts the whole truth—ours is a potentially poison pen.

Harvey termed his "news" as page 1 and the commercial as page 2. In that broadcast, Harvey described a situation he believed to exist, then "commented" on it. He did not issue a call for action, but he did advance a solution to the problem.

WSAU, WASAU, WISCONSIN

The Forward Communications Corporation is licensee of five TV and six radio stations, all of which editorialize. Among them is WSAU in Wasau, Wisconsin. These stations not only have a credible track record in editorializing, but were the first to do so in Wisconsin. Station WSAU was selected for this study primarily because of the extreme conflict that resulted from one of its editorial efforts.

George Bundner, vice president for broadcast affairs, wrote that WSAU's aim is to take a side in controversy—to at least provoke thought, and hopefully to instigate action for the betterment of community needs."

Bendner said WSAU's editorials are not always controversial, "but our intent toward that end obligates us to offer equal opportunity to opposing views. We welcome such opposition from qualified sources. And if we present a personal attack, the subject is afforded an advance copy of the editorial with an invitation to reply."

Each of the seven Forward Communication broadcast complexes operates with complete autonomy in the matter of editorial presentation. The editorial board in each market is composed of five to seven persons at the department-head level. The boards meet regularly, usually once a week, to discuss and outline the content of each editorial. The WSAU operation airs editorials each Tuesday and Thursday in the 6:00 p.m. news block on TV. The same editorials are aired the following day on radio in morning and afternoon drive periods. The frequency of presentation by other stations in Forward varies according to each particular situation.

Bundner said his stations do not use any production techniques beyond the "ordinary methods of presentation." Slides, film, and sound are used when they can be readily adapted to a particular situation. "For example, we recently advocated passage of a school bond issue in a neighboring town for monies to replace a school building. The film showed the bad state of disrepair at the old building," he said. In another case, WSAU did an "on-location" editorial, using sound on film, in dealing with local traffic hazards.

"Down through the years we have had many comments, mostly in favor of our editorial policy. And while we have run into some difficult situations at times from objectors, we have never had any serious attempts to stop us from editorializing," Bundner pointed out, explaining, "Our experience indicates that most listeners are in favor of editorials, even though they might disagree with our views. We think editorializing adds to the stature of our stations; this being another way in which we can help solve problems in the communities we serve."

Station WSAU's editorial of March 11, 1971 stirred up a hornet's nest in the legal profession. There were threats of lawsuits, but WSAU management offered the Marathon County Bar Association reply time, and there the matter was settled. Here is the editorial that stirred up the lawyers:

> Lawyers who wonder why their profession does not have a better public image have only to look at what happened in Madison this week to find the answer.
>
> Members of the legal establishment turned out in masses to oppose a bill which would simplify the probating of small estates.
>
> Specifically, the measure which the attorneys were fighting would allow a person with an estate worth less than $30,000 to make and file his own will—probate it—with the register in probate for a $5.00 fee. Lawyers, who take a percentage of all estates, would not be needed for probate of this kind and, as a result, would not get a fee.
>
> Despite their obvious selfish motive in resisting any attempt to change Wisconsin's archaic probate laws, the lawyers invariably defend their opposition on the grounds that the present system is needed to protect the property of the estate, to pay debts and taxes, and to determine exactly who is entitled to share in the estate.
>
> All of this is well and good. But we've known of too many cases where the legal fees involved in the handling of small estates have reduced the modest estates to little or nothing. Talk to any man on the street and he can tell you of similar instances.
>
> Philip Habermann, executive director of the state bar of Wisconsin, is typical of the lawyers who defend the probate system. Habermann recently described as a major revision of the probate laws some mild changes which the 1969 legislature approved. Those changes speeded up the handling of net estates of $10,000 or less, but they could have been made to include larger estates and to give more consideration to the heirs.
>
> Actually, full reform of the probate system is needed, but we're not likely to get it out of the present legislature.

The Assembly Judiciary Committee, which conducted this week's hearing, was composed entirely of lawyers, and if, by chance, any reform bill so much as gets out of committee, it would still have a rough gauntlet to run in the assembly, where 20 of the 100 representatives are lawyers, or in the senate, where 11 of the 33 senators are lawyers.

Only a massive outpouring of public expression for probate reform will bring it to the serious attention of the legislature, and we recommend that Wisconsin residents write to their legislators and inform them how they stand on the question.

Incidentally, an attorney representing one of Milwaukee's largest probate law firms told newsmen following the hearing: "It's you who are causing the rift between the bar association and the public."

If that is true, then the news media should consider the remark the supreme accolade. The news media would be derelict in their duty if they didn't remind the public that lawyers opposing probate reform are frustrating the will of the people.

Bundner said the editorial brought many favorable comments from the public, "but the lawyer body was at us vociferously with the threat of suits.

The lack of specificity in the fifth paragraph is what put us on the hook. Of course, after it was all over, we received any number of documented cases from listeners to prove our point. One of the problems of editorializing in our case is the lack of personnel and time to fully research some of the subjects we choose. However, we do the best we can, stand by our view, and let the chips fall where they may."

While the lawyers' reply to WSAU's editorial is lengthy, it is an excellent illustration of the fascinating battles in which editorializing stations sometimes find themselves. In on-the-air conflicts of this nature, the public always profits from the information that is exposed. It (the controversy) is the epitome of the purpose of editorializing. It was billed as a guest editorial:

Attorney Herbert Terwilliger of
Genrick, Terwilliger, Wakeen, Piehler & Conway (Law Firm)

In a recent editorial comment, WSAU Radio and TV saw fit to criticize publicly the entire legal profession. It assumed that lawyers were opposed to improvements in our laws, our legal system, the courts, and probate, in particular. This is not true. We lawyers know better than anyone else that there is room for improvement in our laws and the practices in our courts. We, therefore, work constantly through our bar association for improvement and simplification in all court procedures. However, the present probate system has developed over a number of years for the purpose of protecting the rights of the deceased, his heirs, creditors, and the taxing authorities. If all are to be protected, changes must be carefully made.

The editorial suggestion that people can draft their own wills would defeat the safeguards the law has wisely placed upon the execution of a will. Even with these safeguards, there are some cases where wills are upset because of fraud and undue influence.

The formal requirements of determining heirship is to assure that a correct determination is made as to who the heirs might be. The last legislature under the leadership of the state bar adopted a new probate code by which an estate with less than $1500 can be transferred on the affidavit of any one heir who is then expected to pay creditors and share it equitably with the other heirs. A simplified summary assignment of an estate up to $10,000 was also adopted.

Protection for creditors is essential if people who need credit from merchants or banks expect to get that credit.

One of the most difficult problems in probate and the thing that takes a great deal of a lawyer's time is the preparation of the inheritance tax and the income tax returns which are required by state and federal laws. Until those tax statutes are simplified and streamlined and tax exemptions liberalized, probate will continue to have a myriad of problems which require the competent attention of a trained lawyer.

WSAU has charged that there are "many cases where the legal fees reduced modest estates to little or nothing." We knew this was not true.

We asked WSAU to give us any specific cases they had to back up this claim. After repeated requests for names and cases, they finally gave us the names of three cases in Marathon County.

We checked those cases. Here is the truth. Here are the facts. Case No. 1—a joint tenancy proceeding. Amount of assets involved was $17,504.32, plus $15,000 life insurance. Attorney fees charged were $200. No charge at all was made on the $15,000 life insurance. Case No. 2—a probate of will proceeding. Amount of assets involved was $15,087.03. Attorneys fees charged were $188.

It is obvious that the true facts give the lie to the editorial comment. Attorney fees in those cases did not reduce the estate to little or nothing. It is clear that WSAU did not check the facts. They admitted they didn't. They admitted they didn't even bother to investigate the cases before they published their editorial.

If the WSAU editorial board or, indeed, if anyone else has any genuine knowledge of attorneys fees reducing modest estates to little or nothing, they should come forward with this evidence. If there is an instance of overcharging, it would be handled by the bar's grievance procedures, which yearly results in the discipline of an average of six attorneys throughout Wisconsin.

Now, specifically, about lawyers' probate fees. There is apparently some misinformation as to fees. In smaller estates, the attorney fees range from 3 percent to 5 percent of the amount involved. In the case of joint tenancy, it is only 2½ percent of the one-half interest that passes. For example, on a $10,000 estate in joint tenancy, the fee would be $125. All probate fees are examined by and must be approved or disapproved by the probate judge.

We lawyers want improvement, simplification, and reductions in the costs of our legal system wherever possible, but we believe it unwise to give up proven safeguards developed by the courts over many generations in favor of another costly governmental bureau for handling probate.

On behalf of the Marathon County Bar Association, I wish to thank WSAU-TV and Radio for this opportunity to present the true facts on probate fees.

WMAQ-TV, CHICAGO

Station WMAQ-TV is located in Chicago and is owned by the National Broadcasting Company. R. Dillon Smith is the editorial director and is a member of the station's editorial board. Robert Lemon, NBC vice president and general manager of WMAQ-TV, heads the board. Other members include the station manager, the news director, the program manager and the assistant editorial director. The board meets on an irregular basis. Editorials are submitted for comments and approval almost daily and this process operates without the necessity of meetings. All editorials require the approval of the general manager, or, in his absence, the station manager.

Station WMAQ-TV is one of five television stations owned by the National Broadcasting Company. It began editorializing in January, 1970. The editorial effort at all five is guided generally by NBC's Editorial Manual, which establishes a general framework to be followed by the stations and makes clear that the ultimate responsibility rests with the general manager of each station. The manual is reproduced in this section of the text.

No station can editorialize effectively without a sound, well developed editorial policy. The decision to broadcast management opinion must be supported by able personnel whose sense of community will compel them to dig into community problems and then offer solutions to solve or help solve those problems. Dillon Smith expresses the philosophy:

"I personally think that one of our functions is to raise a little hell, to keep the pressure on government officials and others and to encourage our viewers to exercise their lung power, too. We think it is important to generate public response, to go beyond merely giving our opinion on the air because that often is insufficient to bring about real change."

In his commentary, Smith quoted a Chicago newspaper editorial writer as admitting that "his editorials from past years do not seem very forward-thinking now; that they really were quite conservative and protective of establishment thinking." The newspaperman's thesis was that editorials must partially reflect accepted ideas—the conventional wisdom of their time. He suggested that his newspaper would have been less effective editorially if it had taken more radical positions, because that would have offended readers who might have chosen no longer to read the editorials and maybe even stop buying the paper.

Smith said, "I certainly do not accept that conservative approach. It is far better, I think, to make waves when waves are called for. If something is right, advocate that without considering how many readers or viewers might be offended. Do not compromise on principles. If we present dull, insipid, meaningless editorials, no one will pay any attention and we might as well use that broadcast time for something better. Not every editorial can stir our viewers into fury, for sometimes we simply try to explain something we consider significant, to let the viewers know they should be concerned about an issue.

"I think the success we have had at raising some havoc has established that this station's editorials are forthright expressions of opinion and so our viewers may be less likely to ignore them even when they deal with a light subject in a humorous way. I would not want to use the light treatment if we did not also treat more serious issues honestly and frankly."

Most of WMAQ-TV's editorials are aired three times: at the conclusion of the noon news, the 5 p.m. news, and at midnight. The same schedule is used for any rebuttals that may be aired. When a subject is considered to be of particular significance, editorials also are aired during the 10 p.m. news when the station estimates an audience of about one million persons.

The station has used several production techniques, the most common of which includes the chroma-key method of visual illustration. The chroma-key method is the electronic induction of graphic materials into the visual circuits. It is considered superior to rear-screen projections and other such early methods. In one situation, WMAQ-TV ran an editorial dealing with the overcrowded conditions of O'Hare Field. A series of 35 mm slides were keyed onto the screen behind the speaker. Some slides showed the overcrowding at O'Hare, while others showed relatively sparse crowds at what Smith called "underused" Midway Airport. It is also possible to use videotape, film, original art, charts, graphs, and any other visual that will help get the editorial across to viewers and listeners.

Smith said his station occasionally records editorials on tape, or films the entire editorial on location. "An editorial dealing with pollution was filmed on top of Chicago's Hancock Building. At another time, we used one of our video tape mobile units to tape three stand-up editorials on busing at three different locations in the suburbs. News film is used from time to time to help make specific points in our editorials—film of people jeering, demonstrators, and sound film of a black woman's reaction to vandalism at her home in a white neighborhood." Smith emphasized that WMAQ-TV carefully avoids doing "anything that might cause viewers to think they are watching a news program rather than an editorial, which is a very important distinction to us."

While the station has broadcast rebuttals, Smith said there were no reactions from any quarter that discouraged editorializing. "I suggest that pressures on a network-owned station in a major city like Chicago are less likely to be effective than those on the local owners of small stations that depend almost entirely upon local advertisers for revenue." This opinion, of course, is contrary to a widely held theory that the richer a station is the more it has to lose via the editorial path. Eric Sevareid of CBS stated: "The bigger our information media, the less courage and freedom of expression they allow. Bigness means weakness."

Station WMAQ-TV, according to Smith, tries to concentrate on local issues because "this is where we believe we can be most effective and influential. However, we do not limit ourselves in choice of subject matter, because all kinds of issues affect people who live in our viewing area. "I cannot overestimate the importance of the way an editorial is written. We try to make it clear and often informal, realizing that most viewers see an editorial only once and possibly then with a lot less than total attention." The station aired 132 editorials and 50 rebuttals in 1971, and Smith said he expected an even greater number in years following.

In mid-1972, Smith published for the editorial board the following summary of the station's editorial effort in a 15-week period:

Local v. national issues

Local, or principally local	36
National, or principally national	11

Length of editorials

Less than 2 minutes	8
2:00 to 2:05 minutes	13
2:10 to 2:15	17
Longer than 2:15	9

Origin of editorial ideas

Initiated by editorial director	21
Suggested by other board members	15
(Lemon 8, Wise 5, Trigg, 1, Wise-Prather together, 1)	
Viewer initiated	9
Other station personnel	1
News department	1

Use of visual material

Some visual or on-location	26
(Some used only simple logos or brief printed material; I figure that 14 used visuals significantly)	
No visual	21

During the 15-week period studied, there were 47 editorials and 15 replies aired, an average of slightly more than four per week. Smith said the low percentage of replies reflects the continuing difficulty to persuade people to agree to air their opposing views. He suggested this reluctance in itself might be a worthwhile subject for an editorial.

Station WMAQ-TV's editorial subjects indicate the station and its management's dedication to the proposition that stations should editorialize forcefully. Subjects have included:

> Opposition to an airport in Lake Michigan
> Comment on the Conspiracy Seven Trial

Recommendation that State Attorney Hanrahan resign after report on Black Panther raid

Call for immediate U.S. withdrawal from Vietnam

Opposition to use of tax money for a sports stadium.

In addition to presenting editorials, WMAQ-TV undertook a series of projects designed to provide its viewers with opportunities to respond to station editorials. The station's first editorial asked for expressions of concern about pollution. More than 26,000 persons responded. Samples of their letters were edited into book form and 2500 books were distributed with copies sent to public officials and pollsters as evidence of public concern about the environment.

One of WMAQ-TV's most significant efforts came in March of 1970. A series of editorials on critical issues facing the nation were aired and citizens were invited to give their own opinions. Viewers were told that a WMAQ-TV videotape mobile unit would be at three specified locations. For three days public response was recorded, then 3½ hours of programing entitled, "What This Country Needs..." was broadcast. The success of this effort led to a series of editorials on urban life, followed by two hours of public response broadcast under the title of "What This City Needs..." A total of 352 members of the public appeared on these programs out of 621 people whose views were recorded.

This is public service! With such policies, with the expenditure of considerable money, and with an intelligent, fair-minded, community-conscious staff, WMAQ-TV-AM-FM should have little difficulty in fending off strike applicants should any ever venture forth. This is substantive participation in community affairs that makes a station **important!**

The editorial series on Chicago's airport facilities is a prime example of the station's alertness to local problems. Here is one of the editorials:

> The Chicago area needs another airport. O'Hare Field is handling a maximum load of flights. Midway Airport is not, but even if full advantage is taken of Midway facilities, we still need a third airport around here. The problem is...where to put it.

Mayor Daley thinks it should be built out in Lake Michigan. We think the Mayor is wrong. At this point in the city's history, we need an airport in the lake about as much as we need sewage in our drinking water.

Right now, desperate attempts are being made to keep Lake Michigan from becoming a total sewer in the next few years because of water pollution.

It isn't going to do the lake any good to stick a big concrete and steel structure out there with jet planes landing and taking off every minute...with a four-mile bridge or tunnel for motor traffic back to the city...and with a shoreline dotted with the motels, bars, and restaurants that always seem to crop up next to an airport.

But the most valid argument against an airport in the lake is that the pilots and controllers are afraid of unusual weather conditions out there.

We don't know much about airports in lakes because no other American city has had this compelling urge to try it out. But the planes could have trouble with fog, with ice on the wings, and with wind currents. And, if the pilots are afraid, the passengers will probably be terrified.

No one knows how much it would cost to put an airport out in the lake...but, even if it was a good idea to stick one out there, it would cost a lot more than putting one on dry land.

Now...about Midway Airport. There are people who say that Midway's facilities are being wasted...and that's true. Midway's a pretty lonely place these days with only 94 scheduled flights a day. The major airlines just do not want to use it. Moving air passengers around the country is a complicated business. The passengers want to go where the planes are and where they can make connections with other planes...and, right now, that's O'Hare Field.

Making better use of Midway could help the airport situation now, but that's not the long-range answer. The accepted prediction is that air travel will triple during this decade.

So...we need another airport, but not out in the lake.

Now...where would it go? There are three proposed sites southwest of Chicago. They are within 30 to 50 miles of the Loop. At first, that sounds like a pretty long haul; but according to transportation experts, you wouldn't be driving there anyway. You'd go to a depot somewhere and ride a hundred-mile-an-hour express train to the airport.

We are confident that if care is taken to explore these three land sites, one of them will prove acceptable.

If we have to keep enlarging our metropolitan areas, let's extend them on land and not into our drinking water.

We feel that putting an airport in Lake Michigan is a silly idea. We hope that Mayor Daley reaches that conclusion soon so that some sensible airport planning can get under way.

Each of the four editorials in this series went beyond criticism of the lake site to offer what WMAQ-TV's editorial board considered to be sensible approaches to future airport planning. Each was illustrated visually to show current conditions at the existing airports as well as the proposed site in Lake Michigan. As Peter Straus felt it difficult to measure the effectiveness of any editorial, Dillon Smith at WMAQ-TV said, "We apparently have not yet convinced the mayor that the lake is a poor place for an airport. On the other hand, nothing has been done to implement his plan in the last year."

Station WMAQ-TV's efforts to preserve Chicago's Public Library Building on Michigan Avenue drew almost 5000 pieces of mail. The editorials reflected research, verve, and imagination. Here is one of them:

    (The following editorial included pictures of the Chicago Public Library, the Coliseum in Rome, the bridge at Avignon, and the Hall of Mirrors in the Palace of Versailles.)

    This is a first for Channel 5 Editorial: a picture of the Coliseum in Rome. It's 19 centuries old, and doesn't serve any useful function.

    But visitors to Rome make sure they see the Coliseum, because that's one way to get a feeling about the history of the old Roman Empire. No one is going to knock down the Coliseum.

    Here's an old building by Chicago standards, the public library which was built 75 years ago. It is no longer adequate as the city's main library. So Mayor Daley and some other officials want to knock it down.

    The bridge in the town of Avignon in the south of France doesn't serve any purpose at all. You can't even cross the river on it.

But it has been preserved so that people today can see the kind of construction the visiting Romans did 800 years ago. If you knocked down this bridge, it wouldn't be a good place for a high-rise anyway.

Now, the library site on Michigan Avenue—that's another story. The Daley administration seems to think this would be a fine place for another high-rise building.

The Palace of Versailles was built in the 1600s for the French kings. France doesn't have kings anymore; so the palace, with its famous Hall of Mirrors, has been preserved as a national monument. It's a beautiful place and the French people are proud of it.

The Chicago Library is beautiful, too. And we're trying to solicit your help in our campaign to convince Mayor Daley to preserve it as something future generations of Chicagoans who haven't even been born yet will enjoy.

If you'll write to us, we'll pass the mail along to the mayor's office. Here's the address: Save the Library, WMAQ-TV, Box 3484...Chicago...60654.

We started this campaign a few days ago. We're now counting mail and we'll give you a progress report in the next couple of days.

We're not claiming the Chicago Library is as historically significant as the great European landmarks. They have stood for centuries without anyone ordering them demolished. It takes time for a building to become a masterpiece.

But just one hasty decision by the politicians...and a few swings of the wrecking ball...and the library building won't be on Michigan Avenue anymore.

That would be stealing a part of this city's heritage from generations of Chicagoans who haven't even been born yet.

Because of these policies, WMAQ-TV has won several awards for editorializing, including the 1971 National Headliner's Award and the 1972 Radio Television News Directors Association regional award for various editorials dealing with State's Attorney Edward Hanrahan and the grand jury that indicted him.

Smith credits the station's general manager, Bob Lemon, with making the editorial policies effective "by having the courage to take unpopular positions when he thinks they are right. He truly believes that a television station has a responsibility to exert leadership in its community." Smith said this was a quality "I find somewhat rare among top management people." Without this kind of commitment, Smith believes "television editorials become valueless except as sops to the FCC at license renewal time."

NBC'S MANUAL ON EDITORIALIZING

December, 1971

Foreword

Broadcasting performs a vital journalistic function. In common with other media of news and information, broadcasting also has the right to editorialize.

NBC recognizes the clear distinction between news coverage and editorializing. News coverage reports and analyzes, providing factual information on what has happened, the context and significance of the development, the nature of the issue, and the various positions on it. Editorializing, on the other hand, takes a position on an issue; it is advocacy and argument for this position by the station.

It is the policy of NBC that NBC-owned television stations present editorials on issues affecting the respective communities of which they are part.

This manual sets forth the principles and procedures for the station's editorializing operations.

I. Responsibility and Organization

A. The responsibility for editorializing by NBC-owned television stations rests with the National Broadcasting Company as licensee of those stations. In order that decisions regarding the scheduling and content of editorials may be made directly in terms of the community served by each station, the general manager in each locality shall have responsibility for the day-to-day decisions.

B. The general manager shall establish an editorial board to assist in the conduct of this function. Normally, the editorial board should consist of the general manager, the station manager, director of local television news, the editorial writer, and such other personnel as may be designated by the general manager.

C. The general manager and the editorial board shall be responsible for maintaining the highest editorial standards. The editorial board shall assist the general manager in considering and selecting editorial topics; formulating the station's position on specific issues; and evaluating editorial performance and results. It shall meet regularly on a schedule consistent with the frequency with which editorials are broadcast.

D. Wherever possible, the general manager shall read and approve each editorial prior to broadcast. When that is not possible, this shall be done by the station manager.

E. Each NBC-owned television station shall establish an editorial staff, completely separate from the news staff, of a size, composition, and competence to develop editorial subjects of interest and concern to the community; conduct research on these subjects; verify all factual references in the editorials; and assist in the preparation of editorials.

F. Where it is believed that legal questions may be presented, editorials shall be reviewed by the NBC Law Department in advance of broadcast.

II. Editorial Content

A. Editorials may be presented on any subject that, in the judgment of the general manager and the editorial board, relates to issues of public concern in the community served, including referenda and other questions placed on the ballot. For the present, however, editorials on NBC-owned stations shall not endorse or oppose candidates for political office.

B. Since NBC does not use its licensed stations for advocating positions on any issue in which it has a corporate or business interest, as a general rule station editorials will not be presented on controversial issues relating to NBC itself or to the broadcasting industry. However, there may be an exceptional situation in which such an issue is a matter of particular community concern. If an editorial on such a subject is proposed in these circumstances, it must be submitted in advance to the president of the Television Stations Division for his review, together with an explanation of the special circumstances justifying its presentation and a description of the special steps proposed to invite the presentation of opposing views.

C. Apart from the foregoing provisions, the choice of subjects for editorials shall rest solely with the station management. Normally, each editorial shall deal with a single subject.

D. The essential purpose of an editorial is advocacy and argument. Where circumstances dictate, however, an editorial may merely state a point of view, express facts relevant to an event or issue so as to assist the public in adopting apoint of view, or raise pertinent questions.

E. The station's editorial position shall reflect careful and fair-minded study. Controversial subjects should be treated with mature and considered judgment and with good taste. Although editorial criticism of individuals or organizations is permitted where the facts and responsible judgment indicate, editorials dealing with issues in controversy should focus on the substance of the issue rather than on personalities.

III. Form of Presentation and Procedures

A. The form of presentation should make it clear that the editorial (1) is distinct from news reporting or analysis; and (2) represents the views of the station management. This should be accomplished by appropriate announcement at the open and close of an editorial broadcast, both aurally and visually, and by the nature of the set used in televised editorials. Examples of appropriate opening and closing announcements would be:

1. "This is (has been) an expression of editorial opinion by Station————. This station welcomes comments on its editorial opinions and recognizes its obligation to provide spokesmen for significant opposing viewpoints a reasonable opportunity for reply."

2. "This is a———— editorial. Speaking for station management is Editorial Director ————————————————————-TV welcomes comments on its editorial opinions and recognizes its obligation to present significant opposing viewpoints."

3. Opening: "I'm——————— and this is a ———— TV editorial." Closing: "The editorial you have just heard represents the views of ————-TV management, delivered by ——————, editorial director. We welcome your comments on our opinions and encourage the presentation of significant opposing viewpoints."

The opening and closing announcements should be accompanied by a slide: "————editorial." The set for a televised editorial should be different from all sets used for news programing and should include a placard inscribed "———— Editorial."

B. The editorial presenter should have no other on-the-air assignments, to avoid confusing the editorial function with other elements of the station's service. In order to enforce the fact that the editorial opinion is that of the station, the presenter should either not be personally identified at all, or should be identified as "——————, presenting an editorial on behalf of station————."

C. The general manager, assisted by the editorial board, shall determine the frequency and nature of scheduling editorials in the light of the station's overall programing, the nature of issues of community concern and the types of editorial services available in the community from other sources.

D. Editorials shall be delivered from a prepared text, which must be scrupulously followed. They may be broadcast live or prerecorded for broadcast. In the latter case, care should be taken to assure that the position taken remains as valid at the time of broadcast as it was when the recording was made.

E. A copy of each editorial broadcast shall be kept in the station files for a period of three years. For purposes of information, copies of each editorial shall be circulated, following broadcast, to the chairman of the board and president of NBC, to the president of the Owned-Television Stations Division and to any other NBC officials designated by them. The general manager should also consider the advisability of regularly mailing copies of editorials to community leaders. Copies should also be made available to anyone who requests a copy.

IV. **Treatment of Opposing Views**

A. A copy of each editorial dealing with controversial public issues shall be mailed no later than the date of broadcast to any person or group criticized in the editorial; and if no person or group is criticized, then to one or more persons or groups (if any) known or believed to have views representative of those opposed to the views expressed in the editorial.

B. The letter transmitting copies of the editorial to the foregoing shall advise the recipient that the station will consider a request to present an opposing view and that any such request should state the substance of the opposing view and the proposed spokesman, and must be made within a reasonable time after the broadcast of the editorial. It should be made clear that similar requests may come from others; all may not be granted, and the station will determine the length of time to be made available to any particular spokesmen.

The specific period of time during which such a request should be submitted to the station shall be determined by the general manager and stated in the letter

C. Such requests as are received shall be reviewed by the general manager, assisted by the editorial board, and shall be disposed of as follows:

1. A request from one of the individuals or organizations criticized in the editorial shall be granted; the presentation of the opposing view by such an individual or organization may obviate the necessity to grant other requests by persons or groups not specifically criticized.

2. If requests are received from a number of persons or organizations, the general manager may select a spokesman from those who have requested time.

3. The general manager need not accept as a spokesman for an opposing point of view any person who is a candidate for public office and whose appearance would give rise to equal-time claims.

4. Any individual or organization granted the opportunity to broadcast an opposing view and the spokesman for such individual or organization shall be requested to execute an indemnification of NBC with respect to the statements made in such a broadcast.

5. Spokesmen for opposing views should be those representing a significant body of community opinion, or otherwise qualified by background, experience, or personal knowledge to discuss the issue in question.

6. The presentation of the opposing view shall be prerecorded at a time mutually convenient to the station and the spokesman. In general, the time to be made available to such presentation shall approximate the time of the editorial devoted to the subject matter to which it relates, although the general manager shall have discretion to vary this, depending on the individual circumstances. In the event that more than one spokesman or views are provided time, the general manager shall have discretion to allocate the total time made available to achieve a balanced and fair presentation of the issue.

7. The copy stating the opposing view shall be submitted to the general manager 24 hours in advance of recording. It shall be edited only to the extent necessary to eliminate matter the broadcast of which is deemed defamatory or otherwise unlawful or actionable, and the person submitting the copy shall be notified in advance of any such necessary deletions.

8. Presentation of an opposing view shall be scheduled as soon as practicable after broadcast of the editorial to which it relates and shall be made at a time or times comparable to, although not necessarily the same as the editorial.

9. The broadcast of an opposing view shall be appropriately introduced and closed, with language along the following lines:

"In accordance with its policy of encouraging broad discussion of community issues, station———is making (has made) its facilities available to ——————— who will speak (spoke) in disagreement with the (station) editorial recently broadcast on (subject)."

D. In the case of criticism constituting an attack upon the honesty, character, integrity, or like personal qualities of an identified person or group (except for foreign groups or foreign public figures), the letter transmitting the copy of the editorial shall state that the editorial was broadcast over the station in question, shall identify the date and time of each broadcast of the editorial, and shall offer a reasonable opportunity to respond over the station. The pertinent directives concerning compliance with the Personal Attack rules of the Federal Communications Commission should be consulted.

Appendix

In order to evaluate systematically NBC's editorial operation, each station shall maintain certain information on a current basis as to the nature and effects of its editorial presentations, so that such information will be readily available for review and analysis at the appropriate time. Among the points which could aid in an evaluation are:

1. Record and analysis of mail, telephone, and press reaction to editorials.
2. Estimate of size and composition of audience exposed to editorials.
3. Any community or group action taken as a result of editorials.
4. Any formal recognition of editorials, through citations, awards, etc.
5. Responses received to mailings of copies of editorials and requests received for copies.
6. Analysis of subjects on which editorials were presented.
7. Record of requests to present opposing views, topics on which such requests were based, and cases where requests were granted.

KNBC, BURBANK, CALIFORNIA

This National Broadcasting Company-owned and -operated station has the same base policy as WMAQ-TV and other NBC stations. But James E. Foy, editorial director for KNBC, observed that "no viewer of both stations could ever guess that to be true, simply because of the way the policy is interpreted and carried out." Foy felt the corporate policy gives stations adequate latitude to fulfill the editorial function. "The only prohibition which has given us any concern at all is the restriction on discussions of broadcast industry topics. I'm sure the idea for it was to control self-serving pieces (like newspapers editorializing against billboards). The effect has been to slow our reactions to First Amendment transgressions and effectively stop comment on such bits of nonsense as the prime time access rule."

Why should stations editorialize? Foy puts it this way: "First, the FCC wants us to. That has been made clear. So, as the regulated, we follow the expressed and implied direction laid down by the regulators. It might give some editorialists a nice, warm feeling to think they'd make their views known whether the FCC likes it or not. But as a practical matter, if the FCC outlawed editorializing, I don't know how independent a person could be without a transmitter.

"Second, editorial replies give people an opportunity to make their views known. I don't know if the FCC considered that part of things. But we've come to the view that people have relatively few opportunities to talk back. Writing a letter to the editor of the paper gives no assurance that the letter will ever see the light of day. But as soon as broadcasters fall under the Fairness Doctrine, we'll be delighted to have people come forward to present another view.

"Third, simple reporting of the news is no longer enough. I'm not sure it ever was. But all news media should go behind and beyond the news regularly, in some other-than-news format, so people can examine or at least establish their own views by comparing them with someone else's, whose position is consistent. Wilt Chamberlain found out he was tall only when he began looking down at other kids.

"Fourth, not all broadcasters have an obligation to editorialize. A small UHF station, for example, or an unprofitable broadcaster of any kind, should feel no great compulsion to express his opinions. He should do so only when he has taken time to study the facts. I think it was Will Rogers who noted that the real troublemakers are the people who know a lot of stuff that ain't so."

Station KNBC has launched editorial campaigns such as those described in the WMAQ-TV, WGN, and WMCA sections of this chapter. The station has editorialized on transportation, taxation, education, and other major concerns in the Los Angeles area.

Foy, in discussing the role of broadcast editorials, said he doesn't see "any difference in the roles of print and broadcast editorializing. The function and the effects are the same, except for such obvious differences as potential audience, for even a small station, compared to a big newspaper."

Production at KNBC is kept simple. Essentially, the format is a talking head with as much visual assistance as possible, including film, slides, and copy. "I'm not convinced," Foy ventured, "that a highly visual editorial is necessarily a good editorial. Pictures interfere with the message too easily to opt for the picture in all cases. I think visuals should be like perfume. Used sparingly, selectively, and occasionally, they're great."

In the following editorial, Foy himself went on camera to explain KNBC's editorial policy to viewers. This is not an uncommon practice in the industry, but Foy's effort was one of the better examples found in the study.

ABOUT EDITORIALS
May 1, 1972

I'm James Foy with some information about KNBC editorials.

We've been broadcasting editorials and replies for nearly 2½ years now, and we feel it's important for us to give you some background on how we do them.

We want to stress the clear distinction between news coverage and editorializing. The news reports and news analysis you see and hear on KNBC provide facts on what has happened, the consequences, and significance of those occurrences and the various positions on those developments or questions.

Editorials, on the other hand, take a position. Editorials are advocacy. We argue for or against various ideas. And the replies present the other side.

It is our policy to present our opinions on important issues affecting our community. And the subjects of our editorials have ranged from the aerospace industry to ethnic and minority problems, to prisoners of war and children's reading scores, for a grand total of 289 editorials and 104 replies.

We like to think that within these editorial broadcasts, we've performed an important public service by telling you where we stand on controversial issues—and why—not so you'll agree with us in every case, but so you can compare your conclusions with ours.

The questions asked most often about editorials are who decides what the topics will be and what the station's position is. In both cases, the answer is the KNBC editorial board. The editorial board is made up of KNBC management people—10 men and women who meet daily. Other KNBC employees often take part in these meetings. Sometimes we disagree and have to hammer out a position through the give and take of debate.

We're also often asked how we select people to do the replies. We make those selections on the basis of written reply requests, from individuals and from groups. We try to select the clearest, most concise, and most directly opposite view; then we do everything we reasonably can to help that person make an effective presentation.

The results? Well, we know we've interested the public in pending legislation. And we know we've made people at least a little more interested in and informed about the actions of their many governments. And finally, we hope you'll agree that we've helped give you, too, a little better insight into what's happening behind and beneath the news.

No. 412

Broadcast times: 6:55 p.m., 1:15 a.m., 6:55 a.m.
Time: 2:37

In a September, 1972, memo to Program Manager Lee Schulman, Foy did an "insider's" interpretation of the KNBC editorial policy. "We've now broadcast about 285 editorials and some 200 replies. Considering we've done a good many editorials on charities and on some of the great philosophical ideas of Western Man, neither of which are "replyable," that's an amazing percentage." Foy pointed out in the memo that the station sends out printed copies of editorials to 1000 or so persons. "Mailing all editorials and replies to 1000 persons, constantly, on all topics, may be an overkill. On the other hand, it works," he said.

"Another thing we do, not covered in our policy, is to do our best to make sure the editorial reply which airs is as good a presentation as that person is capable of making. Sometimes that's not too great. But it has the cumulative effect of assuring people who might otherwise be wary that our purpose is not to let them make fools of themselves.

"WMAQ (Chicago) does several effective and interesting things we probably should try here. For example, they've gone out with the mobile unit to gather 'man on the street' off-the-cuff commentaries on a few questions of local concern. And, they've appeared to do more concerted, all-hands pushes on various points."

Obviously, the National Broadcasting Company has provided its O & O stations with professional, well meaning editorial directors. Foy and Smith are only two examples.

KNXT-TV, LOS ANGELES

Howard Williams of KNXT is one of the few contemporary broadcast editorial directors who has held a similar post on a daily newspaper. Prior to entering broadcasting, he was chief editorial writer on the late Los Angeles *Mirror*.

Station KNXT is owned by CBS and doesn't have a formal editorial policy such as the one published by NBC. The network obviously has a policy that requires O & O stations to present editorial opinion; CBS management, including Dr. Frank Stanton, has long advocated that broadcasters assume roles of leadership in their communities. Williams said there is no policy dealing with how editorial subjects should be handled. "Each subject is taken up on its own merits."

Station KNXT airs six editorials or replies a week and averages about one reply per two editorials broadcast. Some editorials simply don't generate replies, although Williams pointed out that while it is routine to always try to find someone to reply to a particular point of view, "we can't always dig one up." Regarding production, KNXT uses everything available. Said Williams: "We try to be imaginative. It just takes time. I often ask for special film to be shot to go with an editorial. We provide the same facilities for replies. One time, we turned a film crew loose for a whole day with someone for a reply, with them (the rebutters) editing the film when it was shot. That's going a little heavy, but they knew what they wanted and it made sense."

Philosophically, Williams said the only difference in the role of newspapers and broadcasting in editorializing is the "constant, threatening presence of government." He believes the "requirement to put on other viewpoints is a chilling thing which may cause an editorialist to bypass something worthwhile, rather than get into a mud fight with crackpots or worse." He continued:

"For instance, if you editorialize against the Nazi party you may have to put on someone who advocates exterminating Jews. Fairness is more than fair, too often. It sometimes seems impossible to shake off a crackpot who likes to write letters to Washington, and certainly someone on the scene—the editor—should be able to make that determination without being second guessed 3000 miles away. But that's the way it is."

Williams reference to the Nazi party is not as farfetched as it may seem. In 1945, Robert Harold Scott, of Palo Alto, California, filed a petition requesting that the FCC revoke the licenses of three stations, on grounds that the stations refused to make time available to him to discuss atheism. Since the stations (KQW, KPO, and KFRC) permitted the discussion of religious subjects, Scott felt he was entitled to discuss atheism. The FCC denied Scott's petition, but warned broadcasters that they could not deny time to persons who hold a "high degree of unpopularity."

Williams regards government's "heavy hand in broadcasting as the greatest threat to democracy I know. It has been snowballing a lot in the few years I've been here and grows ever worse, all in the name of making us fair. It's insanity."

The quality of editorials written and aired by KNXT requires extensive research. Williams said the station has "no taboos and we tackle anything, although we try to be local and current, which takes a lot of work." An example of digging research and thoughtful presentation may be found in KNXT's treatment of a proposed amendment to the California constitution.

The proposal failed, but Williams declined to take any credit for the negative votes. The editorial is an example of how stations with skilled personnel can interpret the fine print and get to the heart of the question. Here is the editorial:

KNXT Editorial
Subject: Vote No on Prop. 18, the Obscenity Initiative

Broadcast: September 20 and 21, 1972

It's remarkable how, within the past few years, we've become almost an "anything goes" society.
It's small wonder that a lot of people are worried about where it all is going, and want to slow down. The unfortunate thing is that the person who objects to raw pornography as an affront to civilized society may go so far the other way that the Constitution is trampled.
Such a plan is Proposition 18 on the November ballot—the Obscenity Initiative. It's a bad case of overkill.
The opponents point out that if Proposition 18 passed, movies like "French Connection," and "Butch Cassidy" and even "Patton" could not be shown. Magazines like **Esquire, Cosmopolitan,** and even **Time** magazine could be banned from newsstands.
Probably the most dangerous part of Proposition 18 is its effort to apply local community standards to pornography and obscenity. Every city and county could lay out its own rules. What Santa Ana prohibited might be perfectly legal in Azusa. A theater in unincorporated territory could show only what was acceptable to the people within a 10-mile radius. That would be the "community."
The way would be clear to set up little censorship boards all over the state.
There is a need for certain types of control. This proposition would try to protect children from pornography, but it would do so by placing any bookseller in peril unless he knew what was on every page of everything he sold. If the neighborhood censorship board found a bad word, he'd be subject to a fine or jail.
Proposition 18 is full of good intentions—thousands of words of good intentions—but they should not be locked in the Constitution.
Unless you want your city council or your board of supervisors, or their censorship boards, to decide what's good for you to see, vote no on Proposition 18.

Unlike the NBC station, KNXT feels free to tackle subjects affecting the broadcast industry. An editorial criticizing a judge's order censoring the news media for its coverage of a criminal trial brought this reply in September, 1972.

Reply to a KNXT Editorial

Subject: Reply to an editorial criticizing a Judge's order censoring the news media in a criminal trial

Speaker: Attorney Irving Kanarek

Broadcast: September 1 and 2, 1972

    The restraint of publicity by the mass media in jury trials is not any attempt to eliminate free speech which is guaranteed by the First Amendment, but rather is to protect the Sixth Amendment constitutional right to an impartial jury which has equal dignity and stature in the Constitution of the United States with the constitutional right of free speech. Behavioral scientists tell us that jurors exposed to ghastly, ghoulish, dramatic, gory, and editorialized information inadmissible in the courtroom can never remove this information from their minds. Thus, an innocent defendant charged with a sensational publicized crime may have to spend the rest of his life in prison due to the pretrial exposure of potential jurors to such pervasive publicity.
    The right of free speech does not give one the license to commit libel, slander, use speech to commit extortion, blackmail, or deprive a defendant of a fair trial. That defendant some day, God forbid, may be you or someone near and dear to you.

WMAR-TV, BALTIMORE

    "A study of Sickle Cell disease, which affects some 600,000 black Americans, was presented in a 90-minute special report on WMAR-TV, channel 2, Baltimore, from 9:30 to 11:00 p.m., June 4, 1972.
    "The first hour of the program presented the documentary film, "Sickle Cell Disease: Paradox of Neglect," which was produced by WZZM-TV, in Grand Rapids, Michigan, and which this year was presented the top station award—the Emmy—by the National Academy of Television Arts and Sciences.

"In the last half-hour, six area doctors, working in sickle cell research and studies, discussed what is being done in the fight to conquer the puzzling and crippling ailment."

That was part of WMAR-TV's brief description of an editorial-documentary campaign designed to improve public knowledge of sickle cell disease and to urge greater government efforts in the study and cure of the disease.

David V. Stickle, director of public affairs for WMAR-TV, said that since the 90-minute program ran, "We have had meetings with the mayor, the Maryland secretary of health and mental hygiene, the city health commissioner, and numerous medical experts in the field in order to provide impetus to the screening programs now being set up around the state.

"Recently, we received a letter from Governor Mandel promising his support of our campaign and telling of the efforts of the state to educate the public on sickle-cell anemia. This is an on-going program and we have other meetings scheduled with medical and government officials to keep alive what has been a fragmented effort and was a 'paradox of neglect.'"

Station WMAR-TV has one of the most definitive and unrestrained policies toward editorializing in the industry. "Beyond our on-air occupations with such issues," Stickle pointed out, "We believe that stations should assume leadership roles in their communities in other directions.

"For example, for the past three years we have helped to underwrite the Baltimore Neighborhood Basketball League which involved this year more than 3000 young people in organized leagues in the ghetto areas of the city.

"One of our members, too, was also cochairman of a campaign which raised over $350,000 in private donations for construction of a multipurpose community center in the heart of the ghetto—Lafayette Square Community Center—which with federal funds will be completed at a cost of $1,100,000."

Stickle's opinion (shared by WMAR-TV's top management, of course) is that television editorials should not be presented mechanically, nor as a daily fulfillment, "simply because there is not enough critical material to which we might direct our attention without becoming pedestrian. We do not espouse the daily editorial just for the sake of 'doing' an editorial. Rather, as critical and topical problems develop, we examine and address ourselves to such material."

Station WMAR-TV has a different approach to the editorial challenge, in that it combines documentary reports with editorials, examining a situation, question, or controversy in considerable depth, filming the pros and cons, and then presenting the editorial stand at the conclusion of the documentary report. Some of these reports take up to 90 minutes and are presented in prime time.

In addition, the station does, on occasion, spot a brief editorial position within a news program, clearly labeled as an editorial opinion and delivered by Robert B. Cochrane, assistant general manager, speaking for station management. Cochrane writes many of these editorials.

The sickle-cell probe is only one of several herculean tasks undertaken by WMAR-TV. In January, 1972, the station presented Bars to Progress, a five-part study of the Maryland prison system. Four of the programs ran 30 minutes, while the final wrap-up ran for 60 minutes. The series was one result of a 500-person survey the station conducted in 1971 among community leaders. Results of the study showed an overwhelming concern for crime. Station WMAR-TV executives examined results of the survey and concluded that any searching study of crime should begin at its source—the prison system. This extended, costly program series provides unassailable evidence of WMAR's efforts to discover community problems and then use its facilities to help solve those problems. In addition to the monumental productions on the Maryland prison system and sickle-cell anemia, WMAR-TV has produced:

AFTER PRISON, WHAT? An hour-long documentary on new approaches to the problem of finding jobs for men and women who have been released from prison.

THE GIANT JIGSAW PUZZLE. A 30-minute documentary on zoning.

POLLUTED PARADISE. A one-hour documentary dealing with pollution of the Chesapeake Bay.

LEGACY OF VIOLENCE. A one-hour documentary tracing America's turmoil from the Revolution.

ASSATEAGUE REVISITED. A 30-minute documentary on changes on Assateague Island, a 37-mile long barrier reef on Maryland's coast.

THE CRUELEST GAME IN TOWN. A 60-minute documentary on housing.

Station policy generally requires that each documentary be broadcast only once. However, in several cases, public interest was so great that management consented to rebroadcasts. In most instances, after presentation of the documented facts, WMAR-TV aired its editorial position.

KOOL, PHOENIX, ARIZONA

Phoenix is one of many cities in the nation with morning and afternoon newspapers under common ownership. Both newspapers publish under the same editorial policy.

Homer Lane, vice-president of KOOL-AM-FM-TV, noted that of 33 radio stations and six television stations in the market, "several do editorialize, offering a fairly wide spectrum of thought and comment." Lane said KOOL management "shuns personal attack; we attempt to be constructive, rather than destructive, and we try to present all sides of opinion in addition to our own."

Station KOOL prepares 13 separate editorials per week and these are broadcast once each on the three stations. Lane estimates the editorials draw from 20 to 50 listener letters per week, depending upon the subjects discussed. The station has no formalized policy regarding editorializing. "I firmly believe that every station with the resources to do a creditable job owes it to the communities it serves to schedule editorials," he said. Lane himself voices many of the editorials.

In one week during September, 1972, KOOL did editorials on pollution, civil service, machines, television programing, United Nations, slums and poverty, American Flag, divorce, venereal disease, highway accidents, driving conditions, auto drivers, and, finally, presented in editorial form a letter from a listener. Most of the editorials on KOOL are 60 to 90 seconds in length and are scheduled in prime periods.

The listener letter is a good example of how citizen comment can be used effectively in a station's editorial plan. Lane voiced the editorial:

MIND OUR OWN BUSINESS

KOOL-TV, 9-21-72, 10:00 p.m.
KOOL-AM, 9-22-72, 8:10 a.m.
KOOL-FM, 9-22-72, 12:05 p.m.

We received a letter from E. D. Welin of Prescott.

Mr. Welin writes: "A 'Mind Our Own Business' policy, starting immediately, is my proposal for America.

"For too long we have assumed the role of world protector, advisor, and banker. We have backed this assumption with untold amounts of men, munitions, and money; and there is hardly a country which has not, at one time or another, told us to 'go home.' Membership in international organizations has not kept us out of trouble. How they loved us at the recent Olympics!

"'Mind Our Own Business' is not isolation. We would, through the United Nations, cooperate in the fields of medicine, agriculture, environment, space exploration, and pursuits of like nature.

"'Mind Our Own Business' would absolutely end all commitments for military aid in men, money, and equipment. Bombing has proved to be inhumane and idiotic with no apparent results.

"'Mind Our Own Business' would mean that our only military activity would be the building of a defense second to none.

"'Mind Our Own Business' means we would show the world that democracy is the best known form of government."

So wrote E. D. Welin of Prescott, Arizona.

KIRO, SEATTLE

KIRO Radio and Television has one of the few editorial policies that does not relate editorializing to the desires or rules of the FCC. Editorial Director Charles A. Boyle spelled out the policy:

1. We believe that freedom is a divine gift of a Creator who intended men to govern themselves.
2. We believe that the United States was established with Divine help to stand as a bastion of freedom in the world, and that its constitution with its three basic departments of government is the supreme law of this land.
3. We believe that freedom can survive only if men care for it, and nourish freedom with knowledge and understanding. Freedom cannot survive in the dark soil of ignorance and apathy.
4. We believe that self-government depends upon vigorous and informed conviction, and this can be encouraged only by free exchange of opinion.
5. We believe that the important and rapidly growing broadcast industry has a basic responsibility to nurture freedom and strengthen self-government; first, by impartially reporting the news, and then by offering its own and other considered opinions to stimulate informed discussion.
6. We believe that broadcasting stations should be operated on a nonpartisan basis, with a desire to provide equal time to opponents and proponents on all questions that are worthy of public discussion on such media of communication.

The statement of "why KIRO editorializes" continues: "So, those of us privileged to operate KIRO accept the responsibility of forthrightly stating our opinion, and encouraging the expression of other opinions as an important function of the democratic process. We do so, hoping never to offend by abusive or unfair expression, but fully expecting frequent disagreement. In fact, we encourage it, and will welcome our listeners' frank opinions. We will broadcast other views.

"Station KIRO editorials do not represent only the opinions of the men who voice them. They are the products of careful and timely group discussions and thorough research. We intend to support no political party, no specific candidate, no particular party platform. But we intend to comment as competently and pointedly as we can on individual issues as they arise on a strongly nonpartisan basis. If, on occasion, we stub our toe, we trust that KIRO viewers and listeners will know that it has been done in a sincere and honest effort to promote the public good. Silence might seem safer. But America was not built by taking what seemed the safe course. The same principles of freedom of thought and vigorous examination of issues that lie at the foundation of our American liberties are no less vital today. Those of us charged with the operation of KIRO are happy to accept the responsibility of contributing to the continual examination of those great principles."

Station KIRO airs editorials every day on both stations. Most of them are produced in the studio, but management has on occasion directed crews to do "on-location" editorials. Boyle said, "We have also traveled to every part of the world—Russia, Vietnam, Alaska, Europe, the Middle East—to do editorials on location."

Although KIRO has had substantial response from the public and from government officials, "none of it, no matter how blistering, has discouraged our intent to continue editorializing."

KTVU, SAN FRANCISCO-OAKLAND

Deacon Anderson, editorial director for KTVU, believes his station has lost some sponsors as a result of editorials "that criticized their products or policies." Anderson said KTVU management believes in broadcast editorials.

"We editorialize to cause change, to stimulate thinking, to point out a deficiency and, rarely, to recognize superior efforts. We emphasize local subjects. And we feel that broadcast editorials have more impact (but with less glory) than newspaper editorials.

Station KTVU editorials generally run one minute or less. One editorial is prepared daily and it is run at five different times: morning, noon, late afternoon, mid-prime time, and after the news. No editorial comment is permitted inside the news and editorials are clearly set apart.

"We feel an obligation to be involved in those activities which grew naturally out of our information-collecting capabilities. Editorials are the mandatory response to much of what we see and hear in the news," Anderson said.

"Editorials should be approached frankly, honestly, without any regard whatever for political or commercial involvement. And at KTVU they are approached in just that way," he declared.

Station KTVU's effort is proof that editorials can be brief as well as effective. This attack on congress is offered as evidence:

> Outlook: No 49er-Ram Game
> Playdate: September 7-8, 1972.
>
> This Friday night, for the first time in years, we will not be bringing you the football game between the 49ers and the Rams.
> We want to bring it to you and the teams would like us to, and we know that you want to see it. But there is an absurd little law that prohibits us from bringing you professional football if there is a high school game in our prime viewing area.
> There is a parochial school exhibition football game. The schools have said that they don't mind if we bring you the pro game.
> But we can't. It's against the law. Now there's something to write your congressman about, because congress passed that law.

WGN, CHICAGO

One of the nation's oldest and most formidable broadcast operations has a plain-worded editorial policy.

> We address ourselves to the
> problems of our community, our
> region, our state, our nation.

Bob Manewith, editorial director, said WGN has little written policy regarding editorializing beyond that simple statement. "We have a stated policy to broadcast editorials and to provide opportunity for those whose views are different from our own to make their divergent statements over WGN's facilities," he said.

Station WGN's organizational technique makes maximum use of station talent with a minimum expense directly related to the editorial effort. The "department" consists of Manewith and one assistant. But the department draws on top company executives for editorial judgment and on virtually every other department for production assistance. Editorial subjects, of course, are taken from news topics which have been researched in part by the news staff members. Manewith himself conducts additional research when required and does most of the writing. His assistant is a trained journalist.

The WGN Editorial Board is made up of eight persons:

1. Vice president and assistant to the president
2. Vice president for public relations and advertising
3. Vice president for community affairs, group stations
4. Vice president for corporate planning and development
5. Manager of news
6. Director of farm services
7. Film director
8. Editorial director

The president of the company and the general managers of the radio and TV stations are exofficio members of the board and maintain the power of veto. Each receives a copy of every proposed editorial before it is aired, but top management is not involved in the investigative and hammering-out process. Good management procedures require that top executives involve themselves in the editorial program.

The board's responsibilities, basically, consist of selecting subjects and positions and reviewing draft texts. Subjects derive from WGN's daily news production, whether suggested by members of the board, others in and out of the company, the daily newspapers, or broadcast competitors.

Regarding cooperation with other departments, Manewith said there is a "certain amount of cross-pollination, either at the level of the editorial board or through generally good internal communications. For instance, we receive many requests for editorial support of all sorts of things and often determine that the subject is more suited to a public service announcement." Manewith pointed out that the subject may have more air plays through a PSA campaign than it would receive in an editorial effort.

Station WGN's extraordinary antidrug abuse campaign is detailed in chapter 7. It is but one of the several examples cited to indicate that time and patience are important ingredients in any massive public service or public affairs campaign. Money, trained personnel, and sophisticated equipment also are necessary for optimum results; but many stations manage a credible effort with only a basic staff and facilities. Many campaigns do not require "special budgets or personnel."

All editorials at WGN are aired on both radio and television. All editorials are taped. Filmed actualities, as well as cartoons, are used to illustrate the TV versions. Efforts have been made to give cartoons movement, with producers relying most often on camera pan, tilt, or zoom, but occasionally using drop-ins and moving figures.

Manewith said WGN has had no Fairness Doctrine problems, due mainly to management's attitude toward replies. Printed copies of editorials are mailed to those listeners requesting them. All congressmen in WGN's five-state area receive copies of all editorials. These representatives are only a few whose names are on a regular mailing list.

Station WGN's "Crisis in Confidence" campaign is another example of an editorial series that is worthy of study. It epitomizes the role of broadcasting as watchdog over government and elected officials. The following editorials were broadcast over WGN Radio in September and October, 1971:

No. 1
Illinois is in the midst of a crisis in confidence. It is nearly a year old now. It started with the death of Paul

Powell, then secretary of state, and for decades a power in the statehouse. The discovery of a hidden cash horde and assets including large race track stock holdings, it seems, was just the start. More recent revelations find that several of the men who shared legislative leadership with Paul Powell, men on both sides of the political aisle, also had large race track interests, mostly purchased at bargain prices and sold at huge profit.

There are other elements in this crisis in confidence. It's been learned, in recent weeks, that many former state officeholders have received large state contracts as soon as they left office. In many cases, they were involved in the same areas they had just left.

The crisis of confidence in public officials focuses in two areas. First, there is the matter of ethics, conflict of interest, and outside income. It's no longer limited to public officials. Second, there's the racing industry, whether it is to continue in Illinois, and under what controls.

In succeeding editorials, we will make specific suggestions in all of these areas. In the meantime, the general assembly must be told, by rightfully outraged constituents, that these matters cannot be swept under the carpet of inaction this time.

No. 2

The general assembly, about to convene again for what members had hoped would be a short session, will be facing more than it bargained for when it recessed at the end of June.

Among the matters left for another time was enactment of a series of bills aimed at restoring public confidence in public officials. The impetus for original consideration of these bills was the estate of the late Paul Powell, the secretary of state who left, among other things, $800,000 in unexplained cash.

In recent weeks, we've learned that a score of politicians were able, like Powell was, to buy, and often conceal ownership of, thousands of shares of race track stock. Purchases were made at bargain prices, sales at huge profits.

What's the connection? Many of those involved were legislative leaders when the general assembly passed several measures to further racing, and race track profits, in this state. And a state board, composed of political appointees, rules racing. These dealings were kept secret for years, mainly, we believe, because this bargain stock rarely was listed in the names of its true owners. Relatives, nominees, and brokerage houses were listed as the owners.

The legislature must approve measures, strong measures, calling for full disclosure of ownership of businesses regulated by the state, and those doing business with it.

No. 3

In previous editorials, we have pointed out the need for legislation to deal with abuses which have linked horse racing and politics in what was an unholy alliance. There is still more to be done.

The general assambly has dallied too long over a new code of ethics for public officials and over a financial disclosure bill for officeholders and those seeking elective office. Governor Ogilvie submitted a proposal to the lawmakers in January. Other plans have been offered by members of the house and the senate.

Basically, all of these proposals call for declaring the sources of all income, official salaries which are public record, and anything else which might help financial ends meet.

While there is no evil in outside income on its face, the public which pays an officeholder his official salary is entitled to know on whom else or what else that officeholder may depend for any other income

No. 4

The crisis in confidence in our public officials, brought to a recent peak in the disclosures that several people on public payrolls had secretly held interests in race track operations, goes a step farther. Comparatively little attention was called to the practice of giving ex-officeholders lucrative contracts. Very often, these contracts are with the same agency, or in the same area of government just exited.

Three things can be done to protect the public, both from conflict of interest and from paying someone out of public funds until he can find a new job. First, the law requiring competitive bids on purchases should be extended to cover services. Second, if a study or other service is needed, then, with the exception of audits, it should be done within the agency by salaried employees who are fully accountable for their time and expenses.

The third thing, and the one we think is most important, is this: No ex-official should be allowed to work contractually for two years from the time he leaves office for the agency which employed him.

No. 5

First reactions to the race track profits of present and former public officials included suggestions that racing be abolished or taken over by the state. Both of these solutions seem drastic to us.

What is needed is an end to the secrecy which allowed the situation to develop. And racing should not be singled out and be made a scapegoat. Ownership of all businesses regulated by the state must be on the public record. Accompanying conflict-of-interest legislation would insure that persons specifically able to influence such regulation would be unable to profit privately from what they did officially and publicly.

As for racing regulation specifically, the method of awarding dates for operations at various tracks should be examined very carefully. At present, the business success of a racing meet can be determined, to a great extent, by when it is held. Since a politically appointed board makes the racing schedule, the only way to compete for racing dates has been through the political system.

While there are many aspects of racing which should be and are regulated, we feel the awarding of dates should be taken out of politics and be put into the category of free enterprise. The people in racing will come to an agreement on dates among themselves, or will provide competition which should benefit the race-going public.

WCBS-TV, NEW YORK

Peter Kohler, director of editorials for WCBS-TV, believes his company's chief editorial aim is "to stimulate thought. And to do that, we think our editorials have to be informed, informative, and to the point. We also think editorial replies are a key part of this process and we make an extra effort—three to five calls, telegrams or letters,—to solicit replies after we broadcast an editorial."

Kohler, whose background includes editorial work at the Charlotte Observer and the Suffolk Sun, said WCBS-TV's editorials generally (1) define the issue, (2) explain what can be done about it, and (3) advocate a course of action.

Richard Jencks, president of CBS' Broadcast Group, explained the policy this way: "The keystone of that policy is that responsibility for editorializing is placed squarely on the local management—that is to say, on the general manager—of each station. This local autonomy is as complete as human organization can contrive. It not infrequently results in opposing views being reflected by the general managers of CBS radio and television stations in the same cities. The general manager selects editorial subject matter, makes editorial decisions. He may, if he wishes, deliver them in person. He may—and some managers frequently do—write the editorials himself; but, as a rule, he employs an editorial staff who researches editorial subject matter and, after discussing it with the manager and being advised of the position he wishes to adopt, writes the editorial.

"The editorial staff reflects and voices policy, it does not create it. However, the importance of adequate research cannot be overstated. The general manager may or may not select and utilize an editorial board of station management personnel to assist him; but even if he does so, the decision is his alone—the board's functions are purely advisory. The editorial staff cannot have any news duties—just as, conversely, newsmen have no editorializing function—and a clear on-air separation is likewise kept between news reporting and station editorials. Skeptics may doubt whether the general manager in fact has such autonomy—whether he can do this without senior management control. He does. At CBS, we do not want to know about or see a station's editorials beforehand.

"I should note, however, that for a long time after we first started to editorialize we did have two important restrictions on choice of subject matter:

1. Until 1965, we did not permit stations to endorse political candidates. We now permit that, and our stations are in the pronounced minority of stations which do so.

2. Until last year we prohibited our stations from editorializing on 'broadcast industry matters' unless the general manager had satisfied himself that, if CBS had taken any public position on the matter, his editorial was consistent with that public position. This still did not require him to clear his editorial in advance, but did impose a restrictive responsibility upon him."

Jencks said the restriction was abandoned when it became increasingly "clear that there were few subjects which could any longer be categorized as solely 'broadcast industry matters.' As questions of national communications policy came more and more to the forefront during the 60s, it no longer was possible to call them 'industry issues.'

"It is worth asking why we should have developed—and augmented—this strong tradition in station autonomy in editorializing. Why don't we, like the Lords of the Press of a generation or more ago, send out to the provinces editorial edicts in the Hearst style—perhaps, like his, with the operative words in capital letters.

"THE ANSWER, OF COURSE, IS LARGELY—THOUGH NOT WHOLLY—THAT OUR POLICY IS A REFLECTION OF THE REALITIES OF BROADCAST REGULATION IN THIS COUNTRY. THE ENTIRE THRUST OF THE FREQUENCY ALLOCATION SCHEME—AND OF THE REGULATORY STRUCTURE THAT HAS BUILT AROUND IT—IS THAT A STATION MUST BE RESPONSIVE TO THE NEEDS AND INTEREST OF THE COMMUNITY THAT IT SERVES. THIS CERTAINLY SHOULD MEAN THAT EDITORIALS ON LOCAL SUBJECTS SHOULD COME FROM LOCAL

MANAGEMENT, BUT IT SUGGESTS ALSO THAT THE LOCAL IMPACT OF NATIONAL ISSUES ALSO REQUIRES A LOCAL APPROACH."

Details on WCBS-TV's presentation approach may be found in chapter 7.

WSB, ATLANTA

Elmo I. Ellis, vice-president and general manager of WSB-AM in Atlanta, and Leonard Reinsch, president of Cox Broadcasting, coauthored **Radio Station Management** (Harper & Row, New York, 1960). In it, they laid down a six-point advisory to licensees planning to editorialize. It is worth reprinting:

1. The editorial should be presented as the opinion of the licensee, and not of a station employee who may write or deliver it. This should be made clear so that the audience knows it is hearing an editorial expression of the station, backed by all of its reputation for integrity, responsibility, and fairness.

2. The persons employed to write editorials should have a strong professional background in reporting, editing, and analyzing news, specifically in the broadcasting field if possible. Editorializing is no place for the novice or the fainthearted.

3. Editorials should deal with issues of public interest; to go through the motions of voicing opinions on matters of little or no concern to the listeners would only make a sham of editorializing.

4. Every editorial broadcast by a station should be labeled as such, and to give it further distinction and importance, it should be separated from other news and program material by an appropriate announcement of introduction and signoff.

5. To make sure that every word is as carefully delivered as it has been written, editorials should be read from a prepared script that has been checked and corrected. It is also a good idea to duplicate each editorial and make it available to interested individuals.

6. Be prepared to allow rebuttal time to qualified citizens or groups who might have occasion to disagree with your editorial viewpoint and wish to express dissenting opinions.

Ellis and Reinsch continue:

"Decide also which of your management officials is to be involved in making editorial decisions and formulating editorial policies. Establish an editorial board or designate one or more persons to be the final authority on editorial matters. Make clear to the writers of editorials the degree of freedom they are to enjoy in expressing their opinions. Schedule each editorial more than once on the air so that your message will reach a greater total audience."

Station WSB-AM, and Elmo Ellis personally, have editorialized since the late 1950s. Awards and citations include the Alfred P. Sloan Award (1965), the George Foster Peabody Award (1966), 12 Freedom Foundation Awards, and a letter of commendation from President Nixon for Ellis' campaign to save the federal public schools hot-lunch program.

Station WSB has not hesitated to voice strong views on the FCC and the Communications Act. On August 27, 1972, Ellis broadcast the following:

SECTION 315 OF THE COMMUNICATIONS ACT SHOULD BE AMENDED

A few weeks ago, one of the candidates for the senate in the Democratic primary based his broadcast advertising campaign on race bating, hate mongering, and vilification.

The NAACP, the Antidefamation League, and the National Conference of Christians and Jews registered their dismay and disgust by appealing to the Federal Communications Commission to put a stop to such shameless abuse of the airwaves.

Earlier appeals by these organizations—and by the mayor of Atlanta—to local radio and television stations had been answered with the explanation that federal law, Section 315 of the Communications Act, expressly forbids a

175

radio or television station from altering or censoring in any manner the content of a qualified political candidate's message.

Congress passed such a law originally to protect the political office seeker, whose views might not coincide with or meet the approval of the broadcast management with which he had to deal.

But here in Georgia, we were faced with a reverse situation, which Congress had not considered: the public was left unprotected against a barrage of insulting and revolting remarks that certainly overstepped the boundaries of decency and fairness.

As a lifelong spokesman for freedom of speech, we certainly do not advocate censorship. Gagging the spokesman of the obscene cause is not the answer.

What we appeal for is a revision of the law that would remove the screen of immunity behind which the political candidate now is able to hide or behave shamelessly.

It is our belief that a person seeking political office should have the same freedom of speech that you have...no more and no less. He should be just as accountable for his remarks as you would be if you spoke on the air.

As the law now reads, it discriminates against you and all other Americans, conveying special privileges only to the political candidate who is free to be as obnoxious, as villainous, and inflamatory as he has the nerve to be.

If anyone should be held responsible for his opinions, it ought to be the politician who invites your vote and support, so that he might represent your interests in government.

Section 315 of the Communications Act should be changed. Fairness and justice demand it.

Station WSB also has taken editorial positions against capital punishment, supported strong action against skyjackers, and given advice on how to foil housebreakers.

Ellis himself does a daily "commentary" on WSB under the banner of "Pro and Con." The editorials are labeled "WSB Viewpoint." Ellis is a skilled writer and speaker. He is author of **Happiness Is Worth The Effort,** published in 1970 by Hewitt House. The book exposes Ellis' philosophy of life and contains many of his radio essays. On human motivation, he wrote:

"Man is a natural mountain climber, not because he likes to climb but because he needs ever so often to win a battle."

Station WSB has no formal editorial policy, such as those of NBC and CBS. Management simply considers the practice an obligation the station owes listeners. Cox Broadcasting is one of the largest group operations in the country and operates broadcast facilities in Atlanta, Dayton, Charlotte, Miami, Pittsburgh, and San Francisco.

WAVZ, NEW HAVEN, CONNECTICUT

In 1959, **Broadcasting** magazine said "it can be asserted with a safe degree of certainty that broadcasting would be enjoying something less than its present stature in the functions of news and editorializing had not an 18-year-old freshman at Cornell in 1935, Daniel W. Kops, become intrigued with the daily student newspaper and discarded his plans to study medicine."

Daniel Kops is president of Kops-Monahan Communications, Inc., of New Haven. He is one of the few broadcasters in the country to enter the field "to try to restore competition in journalism through a rival medium." Indeed, Kops' WAVZ was a pioneer in broadcast editorials, starting in 1949 in the immediate post-Mayflower period.

The **Broadcasting** article continued: As head editor of the **Cornell Daily Sun** in 1939, Kops helped establish a program of university and local news on WESG, Elmira. That summer he went to the Scripps-Howard **Houston Press** as a reporter and then moved to the W. M. Kiplinger newsletter service in Washington just before Pearl Harbor. Enlisting in the Army Air Force in 1942, he became an officer and supervised communications and electronics equipment activities at various AF installations.

Discharged in 1946 as a major, he joined the **Harrisburg** (Pa.) **Telegraph** and spent two years writing editorials and working on the business side, leaving just before the **Telegraph** was sold in a merger. In New York, he met Victor W. Knauth, who had been publisher and minority stockholder in the **Bridgeport** (Conn.) **Times Star**, which also had merged

177

about the same time. Both men were concerned about newspaper mergers and resolved to go into radio to try to restore competition in journalism through a rival medium.

The station they selected was WAVZ, a daytimer that had attracted little audience. The two New Haven newspapers also were under single ownership, which provided them with their mission—to compete in the news field.

The WAVZ purchase in December, 1949, happily coincided with the FCC's revocation of its earlier ban on editorializing. Taking a few months to size up the community and his newspaper opponent, Kops considered these facts: New Haven, with great past traditions, was slipping in its economic competition with other New England cities. Its schools had not kept pace with population expansion and some were 75 years old. The community chest had met its goal only once in 19 years. Downtown merchants were losing business because there were no off-street parking facilities. Postwar population movements to the suburbs made problems still more complicated.

Mr. Kops discerned a general apathy because past efforts at improvement had met defeat from conservative forces. The newspapers, too, had opposed such improvements as parking and schools. He then began airing editorials, supported by research, which pounded on the doors of city hall, urging improvements. Editorials were focused on each of the problems, but their summary was the same: "Things can be done in New Haven."

The editorial campaign incorporated the showmanship, flexibility, and immediacy peculiar to radio. To get action on a proposed veterans housing project that had been blocked for a year, because the city was using the land for a pig farm to dispose of city garbage, Mr. Kops sent WAVZ reporters to the scene with tape recorders. The editorials first carried the voices of the veterans on the waiting list for houses. Station WAVZ then told listeners: "Now let's see who are the occupants of this obtainable land," followed by the sounds of grunting, squealing pigs. After four days, the mayor stopped the editorials by agreeing to condemn the land.

Other WAVZ editorials helped get action in establishing a parking facility, building new schools, and organizing fund-raising campaigns into a federation. Mr. Kops plunged into local politics by supporting, editorially, a reform candidate for mayor. Opposition party members threatened the first day to pressure advertisers into a boycott of WAVZ. The station promptly aired a second, similar editorial and there have been no threats since.

The reform candidate, Richard C. Lee, was beaten in 1949, again defeated (by only two votes) in 1951, won by several thousand votes in 1953, and was reelected in 1955 and 1957 by record pluralities. Mayor Lee became widely known for setting up an urban renewal and other revitalization projects in New Haven at a cost of more than $200 million, all supported by WAVZ.

Mr. Kops is a missionary. His religion is news and editorializing, and he believes radio is the savior which happened along at the right time to fill the void in competitively produced news created by the thinning ranks of newspapers. He appears at large and small meetings all over the country to urge broadcasters to make news and editorializing a management level function to be exercised seriously and often. Station WAVZ has received the Alfred I. DuPont and eight other national awards for its news and editorials.

After 20 years of dedication to the free flow of ideas, Mr. Kops was still making speeches in 1972. In March, 1972, he spoke to the Association of Greater New Haven Clergy about his work as chairman of the Connecticut Council on Freedom of Information. His words point out his genuine concern over government pressure on information media.

"I am sure you recall cases that have arisen where reporters have been threatened with contempt proceedings unless they divulged their sources. We had one in Groton last year. Some of our neighboring states, notably Massachusetts and New York, have passed laws protecting confidentiality and will be back to the legislature again at the next session to work for one in Connecticut.

"What you may not have thought about is why we work for freedom of information, why over the years men have lived and gone to jail and died to protect freedom of communications. "It's not because as a class, reporters and editors are entitled to any sort of privileged status. It's because they are your eyes and ears. The reporters who go to the scene with their notebooks, their cameras, and microphones are there because you can't be. You can't be at the point of origin of most news stories in our complex society, and the flow of news is so great that reporters and editors must choose what is important, interesting, and timely to you. The press represents your right to know about the policies and activities of our government.

"That makes the relationship between press and government an adversary one. You know, we talk at times of the balance of power in government between the executive, judiciary, and legislative branches. But so, too, is there an important and delicate balance between press and government, each staunchly independent of the other, each serving you in a different way.

Regarding government's tendency to withhold or manage news, Mr. Kops related the following:

"Just a few months ago, the John F. Kennedy Library opened most of the White House official files for the period 1961-63 when he was President. That was when our involvement in Vietnam was being stepped up; but as these files show, the administration was trying to minimize public awareness of the activity. The files revealed a deliberately vague press communique on the subject, prepared by Pierre Salinger after a cabinet level review in Honolulu in 1963.

"Here's how a note read on this communique, written on the margin by McGeorge Bundy, whom you will remember was an adviser to John Kennedy: "'Pierre: Champion! A communique should say nothing in such a way as to feed the press without deceiving them'"

This was the beginning and it was the way government continued to play down our involvement during the escalation under President Kennedy, the bombing of North Vietnam inaugurated by Lyndon Johnson, and the Cambodian incursion of Richard Nixon. "There is only one antidote to withholding information. That is a vigorous independent press."

Referring back to his editorial efforts at WAVZ, Mr. Kops said, "Many of the positions we espoused have been different from the approaches of the local newspapers. And, that's a healthy thing. Not because either side is right or wrong, but because conflicting opinions gave you a chance to make up your mind how you want things to be.

"What we have done in New Haven and continued to do over the years has been duplicated in communities over the nation. Broadcasting has been filling the void in competitive journalism. It is a most essential component of the press and entitled to the full protection of the First Amendment.

Later, in May of 1972, Mr. Kops wrote: "I continue to believe that it is in a station's interest to editorialize, and that editorializing helps a broadcaster sink deep roots into a community. And yet, I am troubled by the many obstacles that are being put in the path of editorialists. I don't believe that the situation will be improved by a constitutional amendment; I much prefer the posture of insisting when challenged that we are covered by the First Amendment. If we worked for legislation or a constitutional amendment to this effect, and failed, we would be much worse off. In the present climate, it would be difficult to get it passed. In fact, it might be difficult to get the First Amendment passed today. Certainly, it is urgent that there be changes in the Communications Act. The courts have eroded the Fairness Doctrine far beyond what was intended by congress.

"The immediate years ahead are not going to be easy for any of us in the media concerned about freedom of expression. In fact, the print medium, which on balance has done more to tighten regulation of broadcasting than to affirm its right to freedom, is in for rougher days, too."

To emerging journalists, Mr. Kops had this to say: "Having the right to exercise journalistic leadership involves the responsibility to exercise it, fairly, of course. A right that isn't exercised will disappear. We need to exercise our journalistic responsibilities and we must keep fighting to protect and enlarge them."

Starting with WAVZ, the Kops-Monahan organization in 1972 included WKCI, Hamden, Conn.; WTRY, Troy New York; and WTRY-FM, Albany, New York. Mr. Kops has been a member of the board of the National Association of

Broadcasters and was chairman of a committee set up by NAB to assist broadcasters in developing editorial policies. His committee met with the FCC staff several times in an effort to understand the Commission's ground rules on editorializing. The committee then passed along how-to-do-it advice to other broadcasters through printed material, speeches, and panel discussions.

CHAPTER 9

Small- to Medium-Market Efforts

Market size has no more to do with effective editorializing than body size has to do with a person's intellect. Many powerful, major-market facilities "are too busy to bother" with such nonrevenue-producing activities. Others are strictly in the money-making business and give no effective attention to station-community relations. In contrast, there are small- to medium-market operators who are deeply involved in community life and who use their stations to promote the common good. The hypothetical "wet-dry election" editorial in Chapter 7 illustrates that any reasonably intelligent broadcaster can produce an editorial that simply supports what he thinks is good and argues against what he thinks is bad for the community. There is no magic in broadcasting editorials in any market in the nation so long as the operator makes a conscientious effort to be fair when his point of view is controversial or disputed. The licensee who uses his station to "force" his point of view or the views of his partisans will eventually have to explain his negligence to the Commission, regardless of market size or economic stature.

    Some of the most effective opinions ever broadcast were written and delivered by persons who had a poor command of the language. No industry rule or policy prohibits the use of colloquialisms, poor syntax, or bad grammar in the voicing of editorials. Dizzy Dean "murdered" the language, but he was clearly understood by those who believed he was "one of them." Will Rogers didn't always use fancy or correct English, but he was understood and appreciated. Alabama Gov. George Wallace's use of the language couldn't compare with the expertise of, say, Franklin Roosevelt or Winston Churchill. But Wallace made himself understood, even in such non-Southern regions as Michigan. Good voice quality is desirable, but certainly not essential. What is essential is that the broadcasters have a sincere desire to use their facilities to help their communities.

WNYN, CANTON, OHIO

Donald C. Keyes, president of the Keyes Corporation, licensee of WNYN, presents some formidable arguments in favor of strong, local editorials. Mr. Keyes is a former national program director for McLendon Stations, and entered ownership the hard way. He traded his expertise in programming for loan capital from friends and relatives. This is only to say he didn't get rich as a programer, then buy a station. Canton is recognized as a medium market with a city population of 120,000 and a metro population of 380,000. Here is how Mr. Keyes approaches editorializing:

"First of all, let's deal with mechanics. I keep them brief, two minutes or under. And that's with an intro and close. Secondly, as in any good writing for radio, I keep the sentences as short as possible. I keep the wording as simple as possible, trying not to use 50-cent words when a couple of 25-cent words will do. Most of my editorials open with a strong sentence. I like to think of this as a hook, one that will grab the listener by the ear and hold him through the body of the editorial. I think it's very important in the opening sentence of an editorial (as well as in a commercial) that we grab the listener's attention right off the bat by going in strong instead of using a mealy-mouth approach. Along the same lines, I also believe that the last sentence should be as strong—if not stronger—than the opening line, and I like to occasionally make the closer a bit caustic.

"Oddly enough, it is this closing sentence that often evokes the greatest response from our audience. I can approach a subject editorially and go through it in a rather matter of fact manner, but I make a point to sock-it-home on the last line, and this is when the phones light up. I'm a strong believer in this closing line. So much for the mechanics.

"Delivery of the editorial is also important. I think it should be voiced by management. If the licensee (or manager) doesn't have good delivery on the air, he'd be better off delegating this responsibility to one of the lesser lights in the station who might have better delivery. After all, we're selling ideas in an editorial and we should give just as much thought to the editorial as we do to the commercial when we're selling products and services. I do virtually all of WNYN's editorials because I'm an experienced air voice."

The author agrees that good delivery is desirable and could not see Mr. Keyes arguing any other way, considering his background in programing and his excellent on-air delivery. But unless management's voice is clearly offensive, management should voice the editorials.

"Many editorials have a promotional value. Please refer to the one on vandalism. We ran this in April, 1969. It is strongly worded and I delivered it in a hard-hitting manner. And at the end, we offered a $500 reward for information leading to the arrest and conviction of those responsible for the vandalism. We didn't have to pay the reward, but we were prepared to stand behind the offer. The reward idea caught the attention of a big segment of our market.

"You will see that several of our editorials are beamed at the Canton Repository, our local newspaper, which has operated with virtually no competition for the past 25 or 30 years. There are no other newspaper editorial points of view on local issues available to citizens. It is sort of an establishment newspaper. Now, being politically conservative, in most cases I agree with the positions taken by the Repository. However, I do not agree with its practice of being a bit one-sided in its news coverage and, therefore, WNYN gives them argument when an opening occurs. Here's an example:

> The **Repository** has finally done it again. Yes, after months of playing it straight down the middle, the Canton **Repository** has decided to become bold and daring. In an editorial yesterday, the **Repository** decided to chastise the television industry. Among other things, the **Repository** said that discourteous reporters at the conventions were shoving microphones into the faces of candidates. Since the **Rep** is an old-fashioned paper, perhaps it doesn't know

that microphones are used to pick up the human voice and in noisy surroundings the best place for a mike is close to the candidate's mouth. Then this fine publication went on to criticize the TV commentators' interpretation of the news, which, of course, the **Rep** does every day under the holy flag of printed journalism. The broadcast media are used to this kind of jealousy, however. For years, radio and television news departments have been bringing live, vital news to Americans, while newspapers sat around folding their evening editions which contained the morning news—news eight to ten hours old. But, we must admit, the **Rep** has radio and television news beat hands down in one critical area. You can wrap your garbage in the **Rep**.

"By the way, this makes them livid at the local newspaper. As I said, they've never taken advantage of the offer to reply. They just sit down there and get purple in the face.

"One of WNYN's editorials involved a sponsor. We ran it in March, 1973, and it dealt with questionable advertising. It is longer than most, but I believe the length is justified:

> We here at WNYN operate with monies received from advertisers. Advertising is an important business quite necessary to the economic growth of our country and is a vital extension of our free enterprise system. Recently, advertising has come under fire from persons who feel that it should be radically modified. Most of the time, we do not agree with this criticism. However, currently running on local radio stations and in the local newspaper is a series of ads that we feel represent some of the abuses that can be attributed to our profession. These are the ads and commercials for Thistledown Racetrack. The main thrust of these ads is to encourage employees to lie to their employers so that they can spend an afternoon at the racetrack. We recognize that the operators of the race track operate under severe legal restrictions that hamper them in their efforts to compete for their share of the entertainment business. Further, we applaud their efforts to get those restrictions as they apply to Sunday racing, and so forth, modified. However, we can see no justification for anyone to tell another person to tell a lie and take unauthorized time from their job for any purpose, much

less for spending the afternoon at the track. We call on Thistledown Racetrack to modify their advertising and take a positive stance in the selling of their product. We at WNYN will not run these commercials, even if given the opportunity. We will not run any commercials that we deem to be immoral or unethical. Further, we call upon our brothers in the advertising profession to consider this action we are taking because continuing to encourage this sort of activity on the part of employees would only work to the detriment of the economy and of our advertising profession. No doubt this editorial will make us unpopular with the Thistledown folks and their advertising agency, but those are the breaks. Once in a while you've gotta rear up on your hind legs and tell it like it is.

Copies of the editorial were sent to the racetrack and the agency. No reply was ever received."

In April, 1967, WNYN aired the following attack on the Canton **Repository**. Mr. Keyes said listeners responded gleefully with "Go get 'em, baby!" remarks.

It must have been a slow news day at the **Repository** the other day because on the editorial page there appeared one of the most remarkable bits of trivia ever to grace the pages of that time-honored publication. The **Repository,** with bravery that makes one gasp with admiration, came out against a bill that would make the mourning dove a game bird in Ohio. In this shattering editorial, the **Rep** says that with so many other problems needing attention in the state, why is time being wasted on this useless bill? With the same logic, W9 (WNYN) asks the **Rep**, if there are so many other more important problems, why do you devote the editorial space to this subject? With one foot in its mouth already, the **Rep** then inserted the other one when it asked, "Are hunters short of things to kill?" The answer is yes, as any Stark County hunter will tell you. The game bird population around here is extremely low compared with past years. Then, a couple of other statements followed which were equally inane. When the Canton **Repository** comes out against dove hunting, they point out what many people have said all along...that being, that the **Rep** is really for the birds.

While Mr. Keyes takes obvious delight in editorializing against Canton's only daily newspaper, he does address himself to other local issues. This salute to the American Legion is but one example. Mr. Keyes is capable of a very dramatic delivery and certainly employed that talent in this editorial.

March, 1918, and a younger America was testing her strength and mettle on an international battlefield. Blackjack Pershing was the hero of the day and names like Belleau Wood and Chateau Thierry hung over the battlefields like a black shroud. And in March of 1918, 50 years ago, a small group of men got together and organized something called the American Legion. Yes, it was 50 years ago this week that the Legion was born. Since that time, other strange sounding names have been added to the Legion's roster. Guadalcanal, Pusan, and more recently, Da Nang and Dak To. And today, the American Legion stands taller than ever before. In every veteran's benefit, you'll find the fine touch of a Legionnaire who's working for his comrades. W9 pauses editorially this week to snap a salute at the American Legion and to commend them with a heartfelt "well done."

Mr. Keyes, with his flair for showmanship, could not resist airing such editorials. These belong in the "nice to have" category and, if nothing else, let listeners know that the station is sensitive to all elements of the community. In the following example, Mr. Keyes makes excellent use of his strong "opening" and "closing" lines. It was aired in April, 1969:

Last Sunday, as many of us watched and listened to the sad and solemn proceedings in Washington, some mindless baboons wrecked two schools in Lawrence Township in Canal Fulton. Records were broken into, offices were ransacked, and broken glass was everywhere. Classes were canceled yesterday in order that the mess might be cleaned up. What with the increasing campus demonstrations and utter disregard for law and order these days, W9 is fed up. We're fed up with the animals whose actions are bent on destroying. We're fed up with parents who don't know or care where their children are.

We're fed up with the courts who give such children a slap on the wrist and a "please don't do that again." Effective here and now, WNYN offers a $500 reward to the first private citizen supplying information leading directly to the arrest and conviction of those responsible for the damage to the Canal Fulton schools. We've had it with these punks.

Another WNYN editorial with a "hook" opener and a thought-provoking closing dealt with student disorders at Kent State.

Kent State University is not really a day nursery, but it's turning out that way. Pouting, petulant students are upset because the big, bad Oakland, California, policemen were sitting in their playpen. Now, isn't that a shame. So, they reacted...in the typical childish manner that marks immature minds. They protested, they sulked, they whined, and complained. Now you can't really blame the little darlings. Sometimes the sight of a policeman will frighten a little child. Now, big daddy, the head of the University, says that some of them will be punished for their little temper tantrums. And that really upset the little dears. They'll show him, boy. They just won't attend classes. They'll go home to their mommies and daddies, clutching their little pink blankets and sucking their thumbs. And if they never return to campus, who cares?

This editorial reeked of sarcasm and, the author believes, effectively "put down" the reactionary students. None of the WNYN editorials presented to this point has required extensive research. Mr. Keyes' interest in his community, and his daily absorption of things around him, were all he needed to write and air the editorials. The following effort on taxes did require some research. It was broadcast in February, 1969.

Tomorrow, at 10 a.m., at the Stark County Office Building, a public hearing will be held to discuss the proposed increase in the real estate transfer tax. The county commissioners have stated that the County General Fund needs more money for improvements in the sheriff's department and other areas, and have suggested an increase in the real estate transfer tax to raise that money. Local realty boards claim that this is an unfair proposition. W9 agrees with those boards. If the money is to be used for the general good of all citizens of the county, then the additional tax monies should come from all citizens...not just a few. Why should the property owner pay for the needs of a person who rents a home...or a person who lives in a mobile home? The county commissioners have suggested that the funds might be raised by a local sales tax. This is a more logical solution. For to tax a few for the benefit of the general public is discriminatory. As a matter of fact, why not give some thought to repealing the existing 1 percent transfer tax? If it's a discriminatory tax at the proposed 4 percent increase, it's only 3 percent less discriminatory at its present 1 percent.

In this effort, Keyes simply stated the proposition, mentioned briefly the arguments of the principals, then stated his point of view and even offered an alternative. This is an example of good local editorializing. Mr. Keyes likes, apparently, to fly into the face of popularisms, as in the following that was broadcast in August, 1971.

It's a funny thing about statues. Over the years they turn green, or maybe they crack...and inevitably they end up as a perch for pigeons. Indeed, there are statues all over Stark County that people never notice. For this reason, W9 is opposed to the drive to erect a statue to the memory of Lt. Sharon Lane and the other 108 Stark County personnel killed in Vietnam. Lt. Lane, you may recall, was the first and only Army nurse killed in that conflict. The idea of a remembrance of Sharon Lane is certainly a good one. We have no argument there. But instead of a statue that will become just another statue as the years pass, why not take the same money and establish a Sharon Lane Trust Fund that would provide a scholarship to the Aultman School of Nursing each year? With a living memorial such as this, Sharon Lane will never really die. She'll be born again in the person of countless young ladies who will then make their contribution to the living...just as Sharon Lane did as a nurse.

The following WNYN editorial has a deceptive opening, then literally explodes into a well thought-out opinion on politics. It was broadcast in November, 1967.

Autumn is a nice time of year to be in Canton. There's a bite in the breeze and the sweet, rich smoke of bonfires permeates the air. Unfortunately, there's another smell in the air. The putrid, gagging stink of filthy campaign practices. W9 refers pointedly to the postcard mailings by so-called "committees." While these mailings do not openly identify themselves with the Democratic Party, it is obvious to a three-year-old that some elements of the Democratic Party are behind them. An all-time low was reached last week when a postcard mailing went out that callously opened old wounds of Clayt Horn, of the **Repository**. While W9 has no love lost on the **Repository**, we feel that deep-rooted personal tragedies have no bearing on the conduct of the paper. It's a shame that some candidates in the forthcoming election have chosen to be judged not on their abilities as statesmen, but rather on their abilities as mudslingers...or worse. Politics is a dirty game, but these vicious postcard mailings go beyond being just dirty...they're despicable.

WGWR, ASHEBORO, NORTH CAROLINA

Add Penfield, general manager of WGWR, Asheboro, N.C., writes and voices the editorials for his station. Asheboro is considered a small market, with a city population of around 12,000. Mr. Penfield said that because of staff limitations, "we have done practically no editorializing. In our operation, it is necessary for one person sometimes to wear several hats.

"This does not mean we have a policy against editorializing. And we have definite plans to inaugurate an editorial series in May of this year (1973). As general manager, I will be preparing these editorials in cooperation with the president of the company."

Mr. Penfield does not observe the brevity policy articulated by Mr. Keyes and others. But his rather lengthy piece on the Asheboro Municipal Golf Course won an award from the United Press International Broadcasters Association of North Carolina.

Again, the question of "research" is relatively moot in the case of WGWR, because Mr. Penfield is involved in community affairs and draws on his exposure to daily events. Here, in part, is the award-winning editorial:

> This is a WGWR editorial. This is Add Penfield. Asheboro City Manager Tom McIntosh Jr., found it necessary today to issue a formal statement about the Asheboro Municipal Golf Course. It was necessary, he said, because of "rumors of major dues increases and sweeping changes" at the club. Personally, we weren't aware there were rumors. We had, of course, heard some beefs about the raise in rates for out-of-towners. The city manager gave no details of the survey...who made it and where, or what cities follow the newly adopted rate plan. He did not mention that...and this is a private opinion...if one sets out to make a survey to bolster a decision, he can do so virtually in any field and come out smelling like a rose. You've heard a WGWR editorial. This is Add Penfield.

Mr. Penfield's editorial ran almost four double-spaced typewritten pages. It is expository in nature and takes only a mild editorial position. The gentle chidings about the "survey" are about the strongest lines in the effort. But it is not necessary to be as bombastic and incisive as in Mr. Keyes' editorials. Mr. Penfield's explanation of the Municipal Golf Course situation was designed to enlighten, inform, and interpret.

In another piece, Mr. Penfield came closer to a critical editorial in his comments on actor Dick Clark's failure to appear at a bowling match. In this case, Mr. Penfield wore his "WGWR Sports Director" hat.

> This is Sportscope...an editorial glance at the Asheboro sports scene. This is Add Penfield. It would seem from here that Dick Clark...who's engaged in making some sort of movie over in Ramseur...owes something of an apology to the proprietors of the Holiday Bowl in

Asheboro, not to mention the several hundred people who turned out at the North Fayetteville Street Lanes last night, presumably to see Clark topple a few timbers. As mentioned here last night, Clark and other members of his movie troupe calling themselves distinctively "The Hollywood Pussy Cat Five" were scheduled for an exhibition match with a group of Asheboro bowlers billed as the Asheboro Cat Scratchers. The match came off, it seems...after a fashion...with the Asheboro bowlers taking three straight games. But there was a mere handful of spectators around to see its finish...mainly because Clark, the biggest Hollywood Pussy Cat of 'em all, was some 2½ hours late arriving for the competition. The match had been booked to start at nine o'clock and four of the Pussy Cats were dutifully on hand shortly after the appointed hour. Not Clark. He called, according to the management, to say he'd be about five minutes late. It was pretty close to 9:30 then. About 10, another member of the Hollywood team showed up. Not Clark. The management called him. He was tied up in a meeting, he said, but eventually would be there. "Eventually," as it turned out, meant 11:30 last night. By that time most of the 300 people who had come to the Holiday Bowl primarily to see Clark had gone home, some of them quite bitterly disappointed, we're told. An official spokesman for the Clark entourage was apologetic in talking about the incident this afternoon. Clark, it seems, had been called into an important meeting last evening...a meeting which concerned budget matters and the shooting schedule for today in Ramseur. "This is the kind of thing you don't walk out on," the spokesman said. "Several hundred dollars were involved." Granted, such meetings must be important. Granted, that Mr. Clark's personal fortune is involved in the filming of that movie, whatever it is. Clark, it seems to us, owed the punctuality of appearance at the Holiday Bowl last night to the public which furnishes the lifeblood of such fame and fortune as he may enjoy. Certainly, an entertainer of his apparent success has been around long enough to realize this. Clark and his Hollywood troupe have been received by the Randolph County community with open arms. They've been heard to admit this. But Clark's gleaming escutcheon was severely damaged by last night's incident, embarassing as it did the management of the Holiday Bowl, the media which publicized the event, and the general public which, after all, puts meat on Clark's table. All of which just could, we suppose, show up somewhere in the box office...and amount to just a little bit more than several hundred dollars. This has been Sportscope...and this is Add Penfield.

While Mr. Penfield avoids brevity, he does make a popular point in his criticism of Dick Clark. Such an editorial voices rather eloquently the feelings of everyone who attended the proposed bowling match to see Clark perform. Mr. Penfield's effort is precisely what any small-market broadcaster can do if he has the willingness and a genuine social interest in his service area. Mr. Penfield was rightfully indignant on behalf of the citizenry.

The following editorials were written and aired in relatively small markets. None of the stations is famous outside the immediate area served. But because these operators had the courage to speak up on public issues, they are respected by many members of their communities. And because many small-market operators are small compared to older and better established newspapers, the "go get 'em, baby" attitude in Mr. Keyes' Canton, Ohio, prevails generally across the nation. Some of these editorials indicate considerable research was done or that the writer had knowledge of the situation from his day-to-day involvement in his community. The city population figures are estimates based on the 1970 census.

KVGB, GREAT BEND, KANSAS; Population: 16,000

> It takes a lot more education today to get and hold a good job than it did 40 years ago. Various reports by the Bureau of Labor Statistics and the Center for Study of Higher Education at the University of Michigan have made a point of this need. We've commented many times before on what an asset Barton County Community Junior College is to our entire area. There is little question that its value will increase many fold in the trying years to come.

This is an example of a broadcaster using a set of statistics from an out-of-town source and relating them to a local institution. This editorial simply spells out the wisdom of the local Junior College.

KLPM, MINOT, NORTH DAKOTA; Population: 32,000

Recently, the William G. Carroll Post of the American Legion in Minot conducted a vote on the question of amnesty for draft evaders and deserters. Those members present made clear the feeling of veterans who have served their country and are now members of the American Legion. They voted for no amnesty. Last week, Senator Quentin Burdick, speaking in western North Dakota on a visit home, commented on amnesty. If you did not hear the report, let us say, to his lasting credit, Senator Burdick is against amnesty. We applaud this position. This is not the time for amnesty for draft evaders. There is never a time for amnesty to deserters. Never! The memory of men and women who died for their country should not be smirched by making moral heroes of the cowardly traitors who fled to Canada and Sweden from their military units overseas and in the United States...or from their draft boards when their numbers were called. Our country is bitterly divided on this issue, with many willing to welcome back the nearly 100 thousand deserter-draft evaders as deserving of an apology from the country they think wronged them. Others clearly feel these artful dodgers are cowardly traitors who deserve no mercy. President Nixon has made his position clear. If he is re-elected, there will be no amnesty considered untill all American troops...or at least draftees...return home from Vietnam and Hanoi releases our prisoners. On that position we fully agree. There cannot be, should not be, any amnesty, conditional or otherwise, while the war is being fought...while a single American serviceman is in Vietnam or a prisoner of the Communists. Possibly when the prisoners have been returned, and passions cooled, clemency should be considered for draft dodgers, deserters, and war criminals alike, but not now! This editorial was given by Leslie E. Maupin, president and general manager of Radio Station KLPM.

In this editorial, the writer did considerable research. He used a study made by the local American Legion, threw in comments by a United States senator, mentioned the President's position on amnesty, then voiced in his agreement. It represented an excellent localization of a nationally discussed issue. Many small-market operators comment on national affairs because (1) there's little chance of conflict, and (2) information is readily available through wire services and newspapers.

Ideally, local stations would comment almost exclusively on local issues if they are to be a reckoned-with force in the community. But, occasionally, the temptation to verbally assault the federal government is irresistible. Editorials on national situations indeed are proper, just as no newscast can be complete without some mention of the national picture.

It should be clear to broadcasters everywhere that society needs divergent editorials on public issues. Broadcasters must take a position alongside crusading newspapers if ever they are to become important in American journalism. Station WMCA in New York performed magnificently in that state's redistricting issue, a feat at least equal to the Washington Post's role in bringing the Watergate scandal to public view. The day when only newspapers represent "The Press" is gone. Radio and TV stations must pick up the baton of editorializing and run with it. It is not only a right and a privilege. It is a solemn duty.

Contributors

Anderson, Deacon; editorial director, KTVU, San Francisco.

Boyle, Charles A.; editorial director, KIRO, Seattle.

Bundner, George; vice-president, Broadcast Affairs, Forward Communications Corporation.

Ellis, Elmo; vice-president and general manager, WSB Radio, Atlanta.

Foy, James E.; editorial director, KNBC, Burbank.

Harvey, Paul; ABC News, Chicago.

Keyes, Donald C.; president, Keyes Corporation, Canton, Ohio.

Kohler, Peter; director of editorials, WCBS-TV, New York.

Kops, Daniel W.; president, Kops-Monahan Communications, New Haven.

Lane, Homer; vice-president, KOOL, Phoenix.

Linn, Travis; executive news director, WFAA-TV, Dallas.

McLendon, Gordon; president, McLendon Stations.

Manewith, Robert O.; editorial director WGN, Chicago.

Niven, Dr. Harold; vice-president for Planning and Development, National Association of Broadcasters.

Penfield, Add; general manager, WGWR, Asheboro, N.C.

Smith, R. Dillon; editorial director, WMAQ-TV, Chicago.

Stickle, David; director of public affairs, WMAR-TV, Baltimore.

Straus, R. Peter; president, WMCA, New York City.

Taishoff, Sol; chairman and editor, **Broadcasting** magazine, Washington, D.C.

Ullman, Sanford M.; manager, News Bureau, National Association of Broadcasters, Washington, D.C.

Williams, Howard; editorial director, KNXT, Los Angeles.

Wooldridge, Jack; editor, **Nation's Business**, Washington, D.C.

Bibliography

Dary, David; **Radio News Handbook,** 1970, TAB Books, Inc., Blue Ridge Summit, Pa.

Gross, Gerald; **The Responsibility of the Press,** 1966. Fleet Publishing Corporation, New York.

Kahn, Frank J.; **Documents of American Broadcasting,** 1968, Appleton-Century-Crofts, New York.

McHam, David; **Law and the Press in Texas,** 1972, Texas Association of Broadcasters, Austin.

Mott, Frank Luther; **American Journalism, a History 1690-1960,** 1962, MacMillan, New York.

Settel, Irving; **A Pictorial History of Radio,** 1967, Grosset & Dunlap, New York.

Skernia, Harry J. & Kitsen, Jack William; 1968, Pacific Books, Palo Alto, California, **Problems and Controversies in Television and Radio.**

Thonssen, Lester & Baird, A. Craig; **Speech Criticism,** 1948, The Ronald Press Company, New York.

Waldrop, A. Gayle, **Editor and Editorial Writer;** 1955, Rinehart & Company, Inc., New York.

Hearings before the Communications Subcommittee of the Committee on Commerce, United States Senate, 1969, Part Two. SN 91-18.

Index

A

Abortion, critical editorial	104
Accusative editorial	91
Alien and Sedition Art	15
Amendments, Communications Act, political announcements	55
Argumentative editorial	88
Asianism	27
Atticism	27
Audience influence	41

B

Broadcasting, control	17
Butts vs. Curtis Publishing Co.	70

C

Call-for-action editorial	87
Campaign	
—Communications Reform Act	48
—editorial	112
Certification, Federal Election Campaign Act	48
"Cold Turkey" program	118
Comment, libel	66
Communication, voice vs. print	31
Community survey	80
Compensatory damage, libel	69
Conclusion, editorial	57
Consent, libel	66
Control	
—media	15
—of broadcasting	17
—of program content, FCC	51
Controversy	31
Credibility, spoken word	28
Criticism, libel	66

D

Damages, libel	69
Defense	
—libel	64
—partial, libel	67
Delivery	
—editorial	98
—print vs. broadcast	30
Drug abuse campaign	115

E

Editorial	
—board	81
—campaign, drug abuse	115
—campaign, future of education	112
—campaign, redistricting New York State	125
—campaigns	112
—critical of abortions	104
—critical of Fairness Doctrine	102
—critical of government bureau	100
—critical of journalism	101
—critical of judge	100
—critical of newspaper	101
—critical of politician	100

201

—delivery	98
—department	77
—director	82
—elements	57
—examples	99
—freedom of the press	102
—KIRO	165
—KLPM	195
—KOOL	162
—KNBC	154
—KNXT	156
—KTVU	166
—KVGB	194
—length	98
—mail form	107
—Manual, NBC	146
—produced	103
—productions techniques	107
—rebuttal presentation	104
—response	26
—responsibility	42
—small-market	183
—truth-in-advertising	103
—TV	89, 107
—types	86
—WAVZ	178
—WCBS-TV	172
—WGN	168
—WGWR	192
—WMAR-TV	160
—WMAQ-TV	139
—WMCA	124
—writing	77, 96
—WSAU	133
—WSB	176
—WYNY	185
Editorializing	
—decision to	56
—survey, NAB	122
Education, future of editorial campaign	113
Election Campaign Act	17
Emotional editorial	92
Emphasis techniques	31
Entertainment	
—news ratio	40
—vs. news	36
Espionage Act	15
Exposition, editorial	57

F

Fairness Doctrine	52
—critical editorial	102

—effect of	33
Faulk v. Aware	70
FCC control of program content	51
Federal Election Campaign Act	16, 48
Financial pressure	38
First Amendment protection	47
Freedom of the press	14
—editorial	102

G

Garrison v. State of Louisiana	70
Government	
—bureau, critical editorial	100
—control, broadcasting	17

H

Harvey, Paul	130
Humorous editorials	92

I

Informative, editorial	88
Interpretative, editorial	91
Introduction, editorial	57

J

Journalism, critical editorial	101
Judge, critical editorial	100

K

Kansas Rule, libel	65
KIRO editorials	165

KLPM editorials	195
KNBC editorials	154
KNXT-TV editorials	156
KOOL editorials	162
KTVU editorials	166
KVGB editorials	194

L

Legal profession, editorial	134
Libel	59
—comment and criticism	66
—conditions	62
—consent	66
—damages	69
—defense	64
—equation	63
—identification	62
—Kansas rule	65
—laws, origin	60
—malice	69
—New York Times Rule	65
—partial defense	67
—per se	61
—privileged news	65
—pro quad	61
—retractions, use of	68
—statute of limitations	67
—truth	65
—types of	61
Licenses, publishing	14

M

Mail form editorial	107
Malice, libel	69
McIntire, Dr. Carl	46
Media controls	15
Motivation, use of words	24

N

NAB editorializing survey	122
NBC editorial manual	146
News-entertainment ratio	40

Newspaper	
—decline	19
—editorial critical of	101
New York Times Rule, libel	65

O

Opposing views, Fairness Doctrine	54

P

Personal Attack Rule	53
Persuasive, editorial	87
Political announcements	55
Politician, critical editorial	100
Press	
—freedom	14
—restrictions	17
Privilege, news	65
Produced editorial	103
Production	
—radio	112
—techniques, editorial	107
Public	
—affairs department organization	79
—Officer Rule, libel	65
—service director	83
Publishing licenses	14
Punitive damage, libel	69

R

Radio production	112
Rebuttal presentation, editorial	104
Reply	
—obligation, editorial	58
—right to, libel	67
Responsibility, editorial	42
Responsiveness	25
Restrictions, press	17
Retractions	68
Reviews, libel	66
Reynolds v. Pegler	70
Rosenbloom v. Metromedia, Inc.	70

S

Scott, Robert Harold	45
Secretary, public affairs	84
Sections 312 and 315, Communications Act	54
Sedition Act	15
Slander	59
Small-market, editorials	183
Special damage, libel	69
Spoken rhetoric, power of	26
Statute of limitations, libel	67
Straus, R. Peter	122
Sullivan v. New York Times	70

T

Talk show moderator	83
Truth	
—in-advertising editorial	103
—news	65
TV editorial	89, 107

W

Walker v. Associated Press	70
WAVZ editorials	178
WCBS-TV editorials	172
WGN editorials	168
WGWR editorials	192
WMAQ-TV editorials	139
WMAR-TV editorials	160
WMCA editorials	124
Writer-researcher	84
Writing, editorials	78, 96
WSAU editorials	133
WSB editorials	176
WXVR case	46
WYNY editorials	185

Y

Yellow journalism	16

OHIO UNIVERSITY LIBRARY

Please return this book as soon as you have finished with it. In order to avoid a fine it must be returned by the latest date stamped below.

MAR 2 6 1975	JUN 9 1980	RETURN BY
MAR 1 1 1975	MAY 2 1 198_	NOV 1 7 1987
MAY 1 6 975	MAY 2 7 1982	
MAY 1 8 1975		
JUN 5 975	JUN 1 7 1982	NOV 2 5 1987
MAY 2 4 1975	APR 2 2 1983	
MAR 1 5 1976	MAY 1 0 1983	
MAR 8 1976		AUG 1 1988
		RETURN BY
APR 1 9 1976	AUG 2 8 1988	JUN 1 1 1989
MAY 5 1976		
	AUG 2 4 1983 QTR. LOAN	JUN 5 1989
JUN 1 7 1976		RETURN BY
APR 2 3 1977	MAY 2 1 1984	
APR 2 5 1977		FEB 2 0 1990
FEB 1 8 1979	MAY 3 0 1984	
FEB 6 1979		
FEB 2 8 1979	QTR. LOAN	FEB 2 7 1990
FEB 2 0 1979	APR 2 4 1985	RETURN BY
JUN 1 3 1979	JUN 1 4 1985	FEB 5 1991
MAY 1979		FEB 2 5 1991
OCT 2 7 1979	QTR. LOAN	RETURN BY
CF NOV 7 1979	MAR 3 0 1987	MAR 1 8 1991
	MAR 1 8 1987	MAR 12 1991
		MAR 2 4 199_